Managing Climate Risk

Managing Climate Risk

Edited by Adam Jolly

Field Fisher Waterhouse   THOROGOOD

making a world of

DIFF

**Our Energy Efficiency Toolkit is
an interactive resource to help
our customers build their own
energy saving campaigns.**

Clear advice covers the
campaign from start to finish.
Innovative tools and templates
help you get there more easily.

**Order a free pack from
our website.**

ERENCE

Choosing the right energy contract can make a world of difference to your business. On the other hand, so can cutting your energy use. To really make a difference, you need the best of both worlds.

Providing a great range of energy contracts has helped us grow to supply more power to British business than any other energy company.† Customers also appreciate the great range of energy saving options that we offer.

It's all part of our drive to help you with energy.

It's easy when you know how.

market 2007

FOR MORE INFORMATION:
edfenergy.com/business

eDF
ENERGY

Thorogood Publishing Ltd 2008
10-12 Rivington Street
London EC2A 3DU
Telephone: 020 7749 4748
Fax: 020 7729 6110
Email: info@thorogoodpublishing.co.uk
Web: www.thorogoodpublishing.co.uk

Advertising sales negotiated by
Petersham Publishing Ltd
Petersham House
57A Hatton Garden
London EC1N 8JG

A CIP catalogue record for this book is
available from the British Library.

ISBN 1 85418 602 7
      978-185418602-7

Designed and typeset by Driftdesign

Printed in the UK by Ashford Colour Press

Contents

Part 1

The case for action

1 Keeping weather on the corporate radar

"Extreme weather is changing the parameters of risks", says Tim Geyer at ERM.

Extreme weather events causing loss of life and major economic damage continue to be front page news. According to the World Meteorological Organization, January to July 2007 "was marked by record weather extremes in many regions across the world." Inevitably, the associated phenomena are starting to impact business and investments, not so much as deal breakers, but in changing the parameters of risk management and the approaches required to devise mitigation measures.

The debate has changed from arguments about whether we need to act, to how quickly we must act, and to determining the most appropriate adaptation strategies. However, this requires knowledge of how and where a business can be impacted by climate change. To date, only a minority of companies have attempted to quantify the risks from climate change. However, investors are seeking greater disclosure of climate change related risks and opportunities, and it is expected companies that can demonstrate they are prepared for climate change will attract higher market valuations.

In terms of typical physical risk issues, companies that are heavily reliant on water may find significant risks associated with changes in the patterns and level of rainfall. It some areas of the world, glacial melt water which has provided a source of fresh water is expected to disappear by 2030. Similarly, companies involved in growing (e.g. crops, fruit) may be impacted by the changes in patterns of drought and flooding. What was a once every 100 years event may become a once every 20 year event and such a frequency of severe impact may be unacceptable for the company concerned. The financial sector should a failure to quantify the physical risks as a major deficiency in a company's strategy, as the risks to the portfolio of assets being held as collateral may be particularly significant. Understanding and adapting to the challenge of climate change to maximise any opportunities and reduce an organisation's risk profile is likely to be one of the most important tasks facing companies today.

Examples of extreme weather events

In August 2003, a heat wave with temperatures as high as 42°C (108°F) struck Europe. As summer temperatures in much of northern Europe rarely exceed 30°C (86°F), the area was unprepared for the disaster, and many thousands of deaths occurred. In August 2005, Hurricane Katrina caused catastrophic damage along the Gulf Coast of the United States, forcing the effective abandonment of south-eastern Louisiana (including New Orleans) for up to two months and damaging oil wells that sent gas prices in the U.S. to an all-time record high. Katrina killed over 1,800 people and caused at least $75 billion in damages, making it one of the costliest natural disasters of all time. This was followed in September by Hurricane Rita, which left 119 people dead along the U.S. Gulf Coast, causing $US 9.4 billion in damage. In January 2006, hundreds of people were killed when Russia, Eastern Europe and Scandinavia experienced the coldest weather for decades. In summer 2007, dramatic floods in the south central region of England, UK left 350,000 people without drinking water and many without electricity. Transport infrastructure was severely disrupted. Combined with floods which occurred earlier in the summer in Yorkshire (north England), the damage is estimated to total over £2 billion.

Assessing the risk of climate change

Methods are being developed to help respond to the need to understand and assess the potential impact of climate change. Such assessments may be focussed on physical risks (e.g. which cause asset damage, supply chain disruption and project delays) that arise from an increasing frequency and severity of extreme weather events. Alternatively, an assessment may include regulatory threats which increase production costs such as energy tax, subsidy removal, imposed energy efficiency standards and limits on energy use and emissions. There can also be market threats affecting financial performance (for example, revenue/price changes from changing demands due to emissions constraints), changes in consumer behaviour, and other financial threats such as the cost of borrowing and insurance.

In terms of physical, regulatory and policy developments, an impact assessment should involve a systematic review of the risks and opportunities facing a company based on the current academic consensus on climate change scenarios for different parts of the world. The inputs and outputs from a typical assessment model are illustrated in Figure 1:

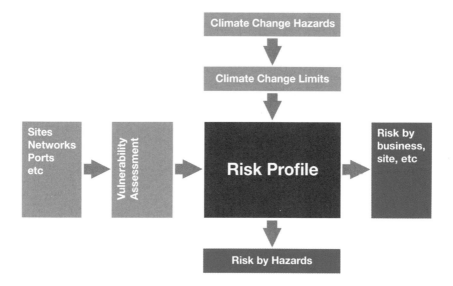

Figure 1: Climate change impact assessment: model elements

The key inputs when evaluating physical risks are:

- The regional location and site specific characteristics of the company's assets and transport networks.

  For example, environmental and operational data about each of the agreed assets/operations, transport networks, ports etc. in terms of their location/climatic region, energy consumption, elevation, proximity to rivers/coast, average rainfall, temperature profiles, water availability, production volumes, transport networks, etc.

- The climate change hazards, for example:

Primary threat	No.	Secondary threat
Extreme precipitation events	1	Flooding
	2	Increased erosion, run-off and risk of landslides
Cyclones/Hurricanes/Storm Events (wind impacts only, water addressed in "Extreme precipitation")	3	Storm surges
	4	High winds/storm damage
Rising sea levels	5	Coastal and fluvial flooding
	6	Saline penetration of freshwater aquifers, rising groundwater
Increased temperature	7	Heatwaves
	8	Increased incidence, severity and geographic spread of drought
	9	Bush fire
	10	Loss of glaciers
	11	Increased number of frost free days
	12	Loss of permafrost/sea ice
Ecosystem adaptation	13	Human adaptation/migration
	14	Distribution of diseases

- Climate change limits based on accepted predictions of the changing frequencies and severities of the hazard events (in a chosen reference year).

Generally only order of magnitude categories are used here, commensurate with the uncertainties in the scientific predictions for specific regions. For example, a 10% increase is risk corresponds to a 5% increase in both frequency and severity, where as a 100% increase in risk equates to around 40% increase in both frequency and severity. However, there may also be similar decreases in risk.

Although some hazards can be addressed in this way, i.e. there is a historical frequency and severity of impact, which can be predicted to change in the future, there are other non-cyclical events which need to be addressed slightly differently. These include rising sea levels, loss of permafrost and loss of glaciers, which are gradual changes over time rather than discrete events. Nonetheless, these can be included in the impact assessment by estimating the probability of a specific impact for a particular reference year.

- Review of historic losses from weather-related events at the company's sites and/or in the relevant industry sector.

    This involves the scrutiny of company and or regional information about previous weather-related events, such as insurance claims, underwriting reports, etc. The purpose is to support judgements about typical business interruption delays, or proportion of assets damaged, etc. It is important to take account of the specific vulnerability to a given threat. For example, a transport network that has already suffered significant delays from flooding would be considered highly vulnerable.

- The key calculation combines event frequency, vulnerability, financial consequence and predicted climate change to determine the level of risk to a company's overall asset portfolio.

A similar approach is taken to evaluating regulatory risks. A range of potential regulatory change scenarios are postulated, with upper and lower bands used to define the changes based on the best available knowledge. The impact of the regulatory change is then estimated for the particular business under study, allowing broad indicative overall cost impacts to be estimated.

This kind of assessment method allows the potential climate change risk to be examined in a number of different ways:

- By business: this would be the sum of the risks for all sites/assets and transport networks associated with each business unit.

- By climate change threat: summing risks by threat would show which climate change threats have the greatest overall impact on the business, allowing common mitigation strategies to be developed.

- By region: this would reveal which particular regions are most impacted.

- By individual site/transport network (see note below).

Note: the certainty associated with the results is generally greater at an aggregated level (e.g. business unit, country, climatic region or threat) than at the individual site/issue level, as any judgments of probability are unlikely to have been systematically under or overestimated across an aggregated group (e.g. business, climatic region).

In order to account for the inherent uncertainty in some of the key variables (e.g. the extent of business interruption per threat or the extent of predicted climate change), Monte Carlo simulation can be used to allow certain variables to be represented as distributions (providing reasonable data exist to define such distributions). This provides an understanding of the variability of the aggregated losses (e.g. for the entire business). An example of a cost probability curve using a log-normal distribution is shown below.

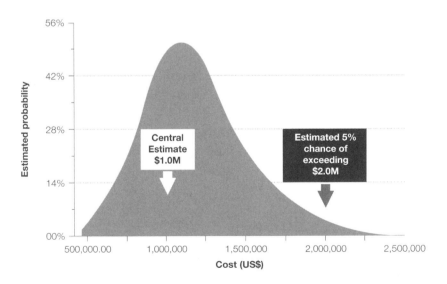

Figure 2: Plotting the cost of an event against its probability

Net present value calculations can also be undertaken to allow potential-losses in future years to be considered in the present day equivalent. This can be important when looking at the costs and benefits of different mitigation strategies.

Increasingly, such approaches are being used by business as a first step towards the development of a carbon risk management strategy. They can be applied using a semi-quantitative approach, relying heavily on the operational knowledge and on judgements of an organization's staff, or in a more quantitative manner, based on extensive and detailed data analysis.

The operational impacts can be converted to future financial consequences – such as increased production costs or reduction in a company's equity value. Furthermore, the same outputs can be used by the operating units and incorporated into their business planning processes to support the medium to long-term business strategy.

In summary, a business which understands the risks posed by climate change to its operations and assets is able to act in a considered and proactive manner, rather than reacting to a serious climatic impact or to the actions of competitors who have acted first and garnered first mover advantage.

ERM's climate change and risk teams offer services to help clients answer the following questions:

- How will climate change impact my businesses?

- What are the key climate change threats?

- Where are the greatest climate change impacts?

- What is the likely magnitude of impact?

- What climate change mitigation and adaptation options should be considered?

Tim Geyer is a Partner who leads ERM's specialist risk management team based in London. He specialises in providing analysis, advice and support to management, focused on discharging legal obligations and improving safety, safety culture and commercial performance. This has included developing systematic risk assessment methods for the quantification of the financial impacts of climate change.

For further information on TORCH and other ERM climate change screening services contact:

Tim.geyer@erm.com

Tel: +44 (0) 207 465 7336.

2 Projections of climate change

Anna Steynor and Roger Street at the UK Climate Impacts Programme present four scenarios on how climate change will affect the UK.

(Text) 'Most of the observed increase in the globally averaged temperature since the mid-20th century is very likely due to the observed increase in anthropogenic greenhouse gas concentrations', said the Intergovernmental Panel on Climate Change (IPCC) in it's fourth assessment report (IPCC AR4, 2007, www.ipcc.ch). The changing climate of which the IPCC refers is particularly evident to those whose livelihoods are reactive to the sensitivities of the weather and climate, but is also reflected in the temperature and precipitation records from across the UK (Jenkins et al., 2007).

Observed changes

As a result of the global changes in climate already experienced, the IPCC assert that a large proportion of physical and biological systems studied are showing a response that is consistent with the direction of change that we would expect from human-induced climate change. To substantiate this argument it is shown that 'other effects of regional climate changes on natural and human environments are also emerging' (IPCC AR4, 2007, www.ipcc.ch).

The UKCIP observed climate trends publication, published in December 2007, depicts the global trend in changing climate (Jenkins et al., 2007). In it, the most widely used indicators of changing climate are those of temperature and precipitation. In this respect, since pre-industrial levels, the global temperature has increased by an average of 0.8°C with the top 10 warmest years on record all occurring since 1995 (table x1). Precipitation in England and Wales indicates a clear trend in seasonal precipitation change since the 1800s. As seen in figure 1 and 2 there is a trend towards wetter winters and drier summers.

Global top 10 warmest years	
Year	Difference from average (°C)
1998	+0.52
2005	+0.48
2003	+0.46
2002	+0.46
2004	+0.43
2006	+0.42
2007 (Jan – Nov)	+0.41
2001	+0.40
1997	+0.36
1995	+0.28

Table 1: Difference from average with respect to 1961-90 (Met Office Hadley Centre)

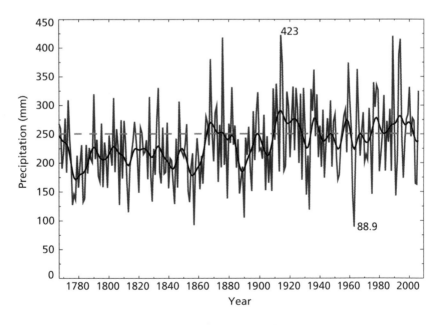

Figure 1: England and Wales precipitation 1766-2006
averaged over the three winter months (Dec – Feb)

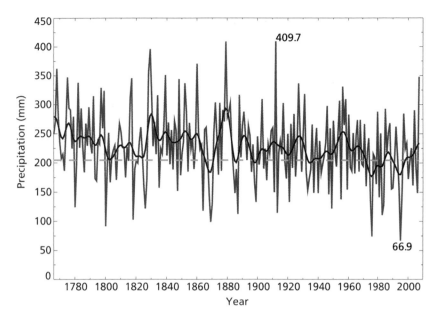

*Figure 2: England and Wales precipitation 1766-2006
averaged over the three summer months (Jun-Aug)*

Climate change projections

These changes in our climate and the associated impacts are projected to continue. This assertion is based on the conclusions of the recently released fourth assessment report of the Inter-Governmental Panel on Climate Change (IPCC AR4, 2007, www.ipcc.ch) and is reflected in the available climate change scenarios from the UK Climate Impacts Programme (UKCIP, www.ukcip.org.uk).

The current set of UK scenarios, referred to as UKCIP02, was released in 2002 and describes how the future climate of the UK is projected to evolve over the course of this century.

The UKCIP02 climate change scenarios are based on the results of a climate model developed by the Met Office Hadley Centre. They reflect the best understanding, at that time, of how the climate system operates. The presentation of the information is based on four internationally recognised plausible greenhouse-gas emission futures for the 21st century. These four futures in turn are based on various assumptions about future human trends and behaviour (such as population growth, socio-economic development and technological advances), and how these might influence future global emissions of greenhouse gases and aerosols.

As such, UKCIP02 provides four alternative scenarios of climate change, ranging from that projected for a world of rapid economic growth with intensive use of fossil fuels (labelled High Emissions) to that projected for a world with increased economic, social and environmental sustainability with cleaner energy technologies (labelled Low Emissions).

Due to the concentration of greenhouse gases already introduced into the atmosphere we are committed to a certain amount of warming. Hence the results presented for the 2020s are very similar across the scenarios and the level of certainty about the projections for the 2020s is greater than that for the rest of the century.

The UK is projected to continue to get warmer

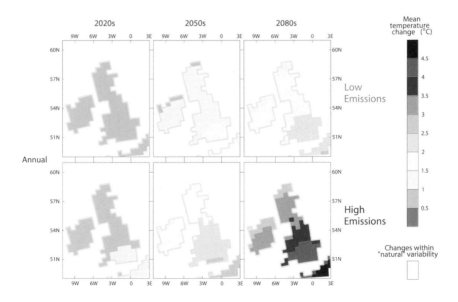

Figure 3: Change in annual temperature with respect to the model-simulated 1961-1990 climate for the low and high emissions scenario

- By 2020, the average annual temperature for the UK is expected to rise by between 0.5 and 1°C, depending on region and emission scenario. By 2100, the average annual temperature for the UK is expected to rise by between 1 and 5°C, depending on region and emissions scenario (high confidence).

- There is expected to be greater warming in the south and east than in the north and west (high confidence).

- There is expected to be greater warming in the summer and autumn than in the winter and spring (medium confidence).

Summers are projected to continue to get hotter and drier

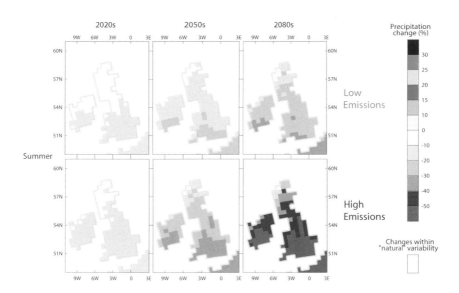

Figure 4: Change in summer precipitation with respect to the model-simulated 1961-1990 climate for the low and high emissions scenario

- Substantially drier summers are projected for the whole UK (medium confidence).

- By 2020 there is expected to be up to 20% decrease in summer precipitation across emissions scenarios, with the south east exhibiting the greatest change (high confidence).

- By 2100, there is expected to be up to 50 per cent less precipitation in the summer months, depending on region and emissions scenario (medium confidence).

Winters are projected to continue to get milder and wetter

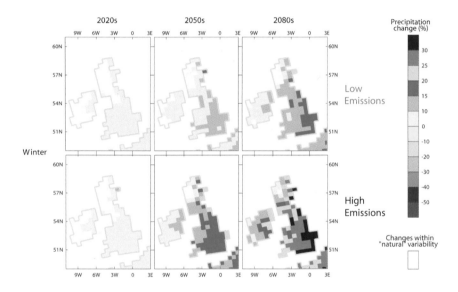

Figure 5: Change in winter precipitation with respect to the model-simulated 1961-1990 climate for the low and high emissions scenario

- Generally wetter winters are projected for the whole of the UK (high confidence)

- By 2020 there is expected to be up to 10% increase in precipitation across all emissions scenarios with the south east exhibiting the greatest change (high confidence).

- By 2100, there is expected to be up to 30 per cent more precipitation in the winter months, depending on region and emissions scenario (high confidence).

- Snowfall amounts are expected to decrease across the UK (high confidence), and large parts of the country are expected to experience long runs of winters without snow (medium confidence).

Sea-levels around the UK are projected to continue rising

- Global sea level is expected to continue to rise (high confidence), and by 2100 it could have risen by as much as 80cm around the UK coast, depending on region and emissions scenario (low confidence).

- There is expected to be greater sea-level rise in the south of England than in western Scotland due to variations in natural land movements (medium confidence).

- Extreme sea levels are expected to be experienced more frequently, and by 2100 storm surge events could occur up to 20 times more frequently for some coastal locations and emissions scenarios (medium confidence).

- The temperature of UK coastal waters is expected to increase, though not as rapidly as air temperatures over land (high confidence).

Some weather extremes are projected to become more common, others less common

- The number of very hot summer days is expected to increase, and high temperatures similar to those experienced in August 2003 or July 2006 (>3°C above average) are expected to become common by the end of this century, even under the low emissions scenario (medium confidence).

- Even for the low emissions scenario, about two summers in three may be as hot as, or hotter than, the 2003 summer by the 2080s (medium confidence).

- The number of very cold winter days is expected to decrease, and low temperatures similar to those experienced in February 1947 or January/February 1963 (>3°C below average) are expected to become highly uncommon by the end of this century, even under the low emissions scenario (medium confidence).

- Heavier winter precipitation is expected to become more frequent (high confidence).

- Winter storms and mild, wet and windy winter weather are expected to become more frequent (low confidence).

To provide some context to these projections they can be compared to memorable events that have occurred in the past (Table 2). Assessing the increased frequency of this type of event in the future provides a tangible grasp on the potential future climate.

	2020s	2050s	2080s
Mean temperature			
A hot '1995-type' August (+3.4°C)	1	20	63
A warm '1999-type' year (+1.2°C)	28	73	100
Precipitation			
A dry '1995-type' summer (37% drier than average)	10	29	50
A wet '1994/95-type' winter (66% wetter than average)	1	3	7

Table 2: The percentage of years experiencing various extreme seasonal anomalies across the southern UK for the medium-high emissions scenarios (UKCIP02)

For further information on climate change projections see:
www.ukcip.org.uk

References

- http://www.metoffice.gov.uk/corporate/pressoffice/2007/pr2007 1213.html

- Hulme,M., Jenkins,G.J., Lu,X., Turnpenny,J.R., Mitchell,T.D., Jones,R.G., Lowe,J., Murphy,J.M., Hassell,D., Boorman,P., McDonald,R. and Hill,S. (2002) *Climate Change Scenarios for the United Kingdom: The UKCIP02 Scientific Report.* Tyndall Centre for Climate Change Research, School of Environmental Sciences, University of East Anglia, Norwich, UK. 120pp.

- IPCC, 2007: Summary for Policymakers. In: *Climate Change 2007: Impacts, Adaptation and Vulnerability. Contributiion of Working Group II to the Fourth Assessment Report of the Intergovernmental Panel on Climate Change*, M.L. Parry, O.F. Canziani, J.P. Palutikof, P.J. van der Linden and C.E. Hanson, Eds., Cambridge University Press, Cambridge, UK, pp7-22.

- Jenkins, G.J., Perry, M.C., and Prior, M.J.O. (2007). The climate of the United Kingdom and recent trends. Met Office Hadley Centre, Exeter, EX1 3PB UK.

UK Climate Impacts Programme

The UK Climate Impacts Programme (UKCIP) helps organisations and decision-makers understand and prepare for the impacts of climate change. Based at the University of Oxford, UKCIP was set up by the Government in 1997 and is funded by the Department for Environment, Food and Rural Affairs (DEFRA).

UKCIP offers a range of tools, resources and support to assist in assessing the impacts of climate change and adapting accordingly. Advice and support throughout the process is free of charge, on the understanding that any study findings and experience gained will be publicly available and fed back into UKCIP resources. For more information see www.ukcip.org.uk.

Roger B. Street

Roger is the Technical Director within the UK Climate Impacts Programme (UKCIP) where he leads the Programme's technical and scientific work aimed at guiding impacts and adaptation studies, and at developing and delivering new tools, including the next set of UKCIP climate scenarios. He came to the UKCIP in January 2006 after working over 32 years on climate impacts and adaptation while with the Canadian federal government. This included working within the Intergovernmental Panel on climate change beginning with its first assessment report and leadership of the Canada Country Study. He can be contacted on roger.street@ukcip.org.uk.

Anna Steynor

Anna Steynor works in the Science team at the UK Climate Impacts Programme. She has a wide range of experience in the modelling, impacts and adaptation aspects of Climate Change from South Africa and more recently the United Kingdom. She can be contacted on anna.steynor@ukcip.org.uk.

3 Getting the energy mix right for the UK

EDF Energy outlines how a diverse energy generation mix can help overcome the three key energy challenges facing the UK: climate change, security of supply and affordability of energy.

Within ten years, if nothing is done, there will not be enough power stations or other ways of generating electricity left in the UK to meet the country's demand for electricity. This is called the energy generation gap.

This is in part because of the impact of environmental controls, principally the Large Combustion Plants Directive (LCPD), which limits the emissions of certain gases from power stations. A number of coal and oil-fired power stations will not be able to meet these emission controls and will therefore have to close. In addition, a number of the UK's existing nuclear power stations will close between now and 2016 simply because they have reached the end of their lives.

This will leave a prospective energy gap of 15-33GW by the end of 2015 and 33-52GW by 2025.

Of course, if electricity was used more efficiently there would not be the need for so much. We fully support better, more efficient use of energy but believe that even with a step change in the way we use energy we will still be short of what we need for 2016 and beyond.

How should we fill the gap?

The Government has recognised that to fill the gap and keep the lights on, while at the same time maintaining affordable energy prices a mix of electricity-generating technologies will be required. A diverse mix includes replacement nuclear power stations and more renewables alongside clean coal, gas and much greater energy efficiency.

We agree with the Government that each of these elements has a contribution to make – gas as long as we are not over-reliant on it, coal as long as it is clean, renewables as long as we are realistic about the contribution they can make, energy efficiency as long as we do much more on it and nuclear as a further crucial part of that mix. However, a way needs to be found to place a value on the reduction of carbon emissions that would otherwise be delivered by fossil fuel technologies in order to give investors the necessary confidence to make long-term investments in low carbon generation.

All types of generation have a role to play

We agree with the Government that the solution is not a choice between investing in one type of technology or another – all types of generation and better energy efficiency are needed.

Coal and carbon capture and storage

Carbon capture and storage is a process whereby approximately 90% of the CO_2 emissions released from the burning of a fossil fuel such as coal to generate electricity are captured before they are released into the atmosphere. The CO_2 is then transported to a storage site – most likely a hole deep within the ground, such as an empty oil well, to be securely stored.

Carbon capture and storage technology is not yet commercially viable but, as it has the potential to allow the UK to retain coal as an electricity generating option in a low carbon future, we believe the Government is right to say it should be explored more fully. The ability to continue burning coal would increase the diversity and security of the UK energy mix.

The development of carbon capture and storage is important not just for the UK but also for countries such as India and China that have rapidly increasing energy needs along with huge reserves of coal.

Gas

Having decided that a diverse energy mix is right for the UK the Government must continue on the path to achieving it. If we do not, it is most likely that 'the gap' will be filled for the most part by more gas fired power stations, as they are currently the most economic option. This would mean that the country would be more exposed to gas price volatility and more dependent on other countries for our energy supplies.

An increase in our dependence on gas would also lead to a long-term increase in carbon emissions. Although gas emits less carbon than the closing coal stations, it would also be replacing old nuclear plants which do not emit carbon.

While gas will continue to play an important role in our energy mix, we agree with the Government that over reliance on one source of generation, such as gas, will not allow us to meet our security of supply, price or climate change objectives.

Nuclear

We welcome the Government's decision that replacement nuclear should be part of a diverse energy mix and part of the solution to the challenge of reducing CO_2 emissions, increasing security of supply and reducing energy price volatility. This is a view we share.

Nuclear generation is a low carbon technology. Even when all the processes such as construction, uranium mining and enrichment are included, its overall carbon emissions are comparable to renewables.

There has been a misconception that there is a choice to be made between renewables and nuclear. This is false. We do not need nuclear instead of renewables: we need renewables in addition to nuclear. Building new nuclear will not crowd-out renewables, but it may put a brake on gas-fired generation. There is no doubt that over the next ten years, much of the generation gap will be filled with gas. Indeed, we have ourselves already started construction of a new gas-fired power station at our site at West Burton. But if nuclear can pre-empt some investment in gas beyond that, then the UK will benefit from greater diversity, greater security and lower carbon emissions The choice to make is not between nuclear and renewables. It is between nuclear and more gas.

In fact, replacing our existing nuclear fleet with gas-fired generation would raise the UK carbon emissions by 29 million tonnes of carbon dioxide per year. While this may be only 5% of the UK's total emissions, it is nevertheless the same as increasing the number of cars on our roads by 42%, or doubling the number of lorries. Over their life of 60 years, new nuclear power stations providing the same amount of electricity as the existing plants could save 1.7 billion tonnes of carbon dioxide – about three times the UK's total annual emissions.

Replacement nuclear power stations can be built without Government subsidy. We are confident that the issues can be resolved now the Government has made its decision. These include:

- improvements to the planning process as set out in the Planning Bill

- undertaking the Strategic Siting Assessment process to identify sufficient new build sites to give investors choice

- ensuring a robust long-term carbon price fully aligned with the provisions of the Climate Change Bill

- establishing clear arrangements for operators to set aside funds to pay for the cost of managing the waste produced by their plants

- conducting a Justification process for new nuclear technology

- completing Generic Design Assessment of prospective technologies.

The Government has indicated its commitment to addressing these by taking the necessary action to put in place the policy framework to enable private investors to invest.

Beyond the policy framework which will address issues including licensing, planning and safety, public acceptance will be an important factor in the construction of replacement nuclear stations in the UK. We are committed to maintaining openness and transparency now and in the future. At the heart of this trust is our unreserved commitment to safety, already proven by our track-record of operating safely the largest nuclear generation fleet in the world.

Renewables

EDF Energy believes that renewables too will be an important part of our future energy mix. Indeed, alongside our sister company EDF Energies Nouvelles, we are actively developing our own renewable generation portfolio. This includes windfarms both on and off-shore.

In addition to our own renewable energy developments, EDF Energy also supports the financing of independent projects through the placing of power purchase agreements.

We are also a strategic investor in Marine Current Turbines which is developing technology to harness the power of tidal currents.

We acknowledge that it has been difficult to make investments other than on-shore wind attractive to investors under the current arrangements and support the government's intention to address this. We will continue to work with the Government to develop the new measures they have proposed to ensure that they attract the intended investments.

Distributed and microgeneration

Distributed generation is generation technology that is connected to the local electricity distribution network rather than feeding directly into the National Grid. The term microgeneration describes small scale electricity generating technologies designed principally for domestic use.

The Government has indicated that they see a great deal of potential for distributed generation to contribute more substantially to our future energy mix. We agree with this view, but at the same time welcome the Government's recognition that it is important to be realistic about the overall size of the contribution they can make and its understanding that distributed generation should be seen as complementary to central generation. We will work with Ofgem and the Government to help identify and overcome the barriers to the further development of micro and distributed generation.

Diversity is paramount

Just as the three energy challenges facing us are interrelated, so too are the solutions. There is no one energy generation technology that will answer all our problems which is why a diverse mix is essential. Greater energy efficiency must also be part of the solution.

4 Brand values

"Running a 'good business' is the only way to make managing climate risk mean true sustainability", says Sara Tye at Redhead PR, who has worked on stakeholder relations for Thames Water and the Body Shop.

The biggest challenges most brands face when dealing with issues surrounding climate change are believability, understanding the best approach and delivering. These are all linked to perception, brand values and core positioning.

It is those brands that relate the environment to their core activity for a long period of time that will really give people a reason to believe, which is one of the fundamental foundations of brand positioning.

The Body Shop

The Body Shop built its business around environmental credentials that most critics claimed amounted to 'green-washing tactics'. But now, over 20 years on, businesses are starting to realise that the company's founder Anita Roddick was really onto something and had a good understanding of business sustainability.

Consumers always believed in Roddick, but they also had to take other considerations into account in their purchasing decisions, such as value for money and aspiration. When profits are continually being eaten away by financial and external pressures, 'being a good business' can be one of the first areas to be compromised.

Setting a business or brand up for failure by causing a deviation between hype and reality is one of the biggest mistakes companies can make, as is not taking into account the future, or short-term thinking about positioning. The biggest issue for any brand is its physical operation and the way it manifests itself and operates.

Nike

Nike is a good example. The brand's 'tick' logo has mass exposure all over the world and the leisure goods firm positions itself as the ultimate performance business, one of integrity. But what Nike actually manufactures is footwear.

When consumers, and especially opinion-formers, found out that the 'tick' was being produced using unethical manufacturing methods the perception of the brand changed in people's minds. If they are not careful, exactly the same thing will happen with brands that claim to have good environmental credentials but operate in a way that abuses the environment.

Shell

For years, fuel-company Shell polluted Nigeria and the environment of the Niger Delta. Yet when consumers experienced the brand at the petrol pump the message being communicated was all about performance and fewer emissions. Ten years after being accused of corruption and cover-ups, and spending heaps of money trying to change perceptions and heal the damage to its brand, Shell is only now recovering.

So what can executives do to ensure the implications of climate change on their businesses are not only accurate and on brand, but also communicate the correct messages to their consumers?

Audit

Businesses must use their brand definition work and operational planning to understand the biggest risks and impacts to their businesses and brands with regards to climate change issues such as transport, energy, food, people and travel. When they have carried out this assessment they will know exactly what the biggest impacts and risks are and what will cause the biggest impression or perception.

Process

Models such as ISO 14001 and the European Foundation of Quality Management Model (EFQM) help businesses ensure information is processed properly and systems are set up to improve the impact on society and, specifically, the environment. This stretches from the business plan through to customer satisfaction, which ultimately comes from the brand positioning.

Yellow Pages

Yellow Pages knew a long time ago that its directory had an impact on the environment and that newer forms of 'info-media' were going to provide a long-term sustainable answer to the directory. After auditing and processing all local recycling schemes and the impact of factors such as paper, ink and glue, Yellow Pages invested in a long-term project to encourage the use of technology and ensure that, wherever possible, the directory was able to be recycled. This amounted to a taskforce, brand and product development team and a funded agency to help local authorities. The conceptualisation and development of Yell.com was the ultimate outcome of these measures.

Implementation

It's no good simply paying lip service to the issues that arise from environmental audits and putting a sticking plaster on activity, or using quick solutions to deliver instant gratification and pacify those that criticise. This approach never delivers long-term results and, ultimately, sustainability. Any stakeholder with any intelligence will know that the company in question hasn't really thought about the issue and tried to address it. The EFQM makes sure businesses are really addressing, delivering, measuring and improving everything they say they are going to deliver. Reducing emissions will need to be part of a study to prove that, over time, they are genuinely being reduced. Businesses should treat it just like any other management activity, such as finance – if you want profitability at 20%, you deliver profitability at 20%.

Roles and responsibilities

Businesses must ensure that a specific person is fully responsible for the impact of its activities on society and the environment. Sometimes this is conducted through the corporate social responsibility department, which might be located within another department or, more commonly nowadays, might be a specific climate change division. Research carried out by recruitment consultancy Acre Resources shows that the number of specialist jobs relating to climate change increased by more than 130% between May 2006 and May 2007, resulting in heightened activity within major companies.

This trend looks set to continue, as current market performance and predicted rates of growth indicate that the new climate change sector will multiply by up to four times its current size by 2012. The explosion in climate change-specific jobs over the last three years is also reflected by large rises in average wages in the sector, from £19,000 in 2005 to £45,000 today.

While environmental sustainability and corporate social responsibility (CSR) have been growing in importance for businesses over the last 20 years, the scope and speed of climate change is clearly a serious commercial challenge that won't go away.

Companies are not just doing this to look good; they are doing it because understanding and dealing with environmental issues impacts on all aspects of business is critically important – and if the business is large, the role will also be large. However, in order for a brand to deliver, everyone in the business needs to walk the talk: the biggest hurdle to progression will be achieving real change and getting people to think differently.

Internal communications

Ensuring that everyone within a business understands the issues is one of the biggest tasks. Running the Impact on Society section of EFQM is one of the hardest jobs to fulfil: understanding and demonstrating impact is a tough assignment. Yellow Pages incorporated all areas of its business and ISO14001 was used as the standard to ensure the organisation moved towards sustainability. The Yellow Pages internal plan was treated just like any other stakeholder communications campaign. This communiqué was used as a best practice case study by the British Standards Institution to demonstrate how a business could change perception, attitude and, eventually, action on reduction, reuse and recycling internally – everything was measurable.

External communications

The Ipsos MORI annual survey, *Corporate Responsibility 2006: Attitudes of the British Public,* highlighted the fact that 67% of the general public believes industry and commerce do not pay enough attention to their social responsibilities, which means those that do are not communicating properly.

Tesco realised last year that explaining and demonstrating its environmental policy would not only go down well with customers, but also with all its stakeholders – including the City. Huge multiple retailers such as Tesco can no longer keep on doing what they want without understanding their wider impact on society. The company started campaigning and communicating about all aspects of its business, from product packaging through to carrier bags.

Measurement

Some brands skimp on measurement as it costs time, money and effort, but understanding whether investment in climate change measures has worked is absolutely crucial to the bottom line. Brand attitudes change and measuring this can be as simple as carrying out attitudinal surveys and questionnaires before an activity and seeing if this has moved on afterwards. It can be as simple as reducing stationery ordering through to something as significant as water consumption. Without this data, no organisation can make a real difference. Gut feeling can go a long way and the decisions business leaders make are usually correct, but demonstrating proof of effectiveness to all stakeholders needs intelligent presentation and data.

A smart working, clever, highly frugal brand or business will be perceived as a best-practice organisation and this can only enhance a brand, its positioning and image. Word of mouth and the internet are the conduits for much dissemination of information in the modern world and anyone who feels badly about a business can ruin the brand or chip away at its credentials at the simple press of a button.

We ignore the issue of climate change and business and its potential impact on brands at our peril.

Sara founded redheadPR five years ago with the intention of creating a smart and passionate company of entrepreneurial re-inventors who understood how to identify the right opportunities and deliver the best return on investment for ambitious brands, individuals and organisations. Further details t: 0870 240 5536 www.redheadpr.co.uk

5 Regulatory control and legislation

"Both companies and directors are going to have to be on their guard to stay compliant", warns Sarah Youren, a partner in the Planning and Environment team at Field Fisher Waterhouse.

2007 saw the introduction of a raft of new legislation designed to address the issue of climate change. It is of paramount importance that companies are aware of the new rules being introduced so that they can ensure that their business is and remains compliant. It is particularly important to take account of the proposed changes and the Government's increasing commitment to fight climate change when forward planning for the business.

The Climate Change Bill

Nowhere is the Government's increased commitment to fight climate change more clear than in the Climate Change Bill which was introduced into Parliament on 14 November 2007. The bill sets a target for the net UK carbon emissions to be 60% lower by 2050 than they were in 1990. However, the Secretary of State can change that target figure if there have been significant developments in scientific knowledge about climate change or European or international law or policy that make it appropriate to do so, which means that there is potential for an even greater cut in carbon emissions to be required.

The carbon budget

The Secretary of State must set budgets for the amount of net UK carbon emissions for each five year period beginning 2008-2012. This will be known as the carbon budget. The Secretary of State must ensure that the carbon budget is not exceeded. This requirement will inevitably provide the legal and political impetus for ever increasing regulatory control over carbon emissions in order to ensure that the target is met.

In setting the budget the Secretary of State must take into account scientific knowledge about climate change, technology relevant to climate change, economic circumstances and the likely impact of the decision on the economy and competitiveness of particular sectors of the economy, fiscal circumstances and the likely impact of the decision on taxation, public spending and public borrowing, social circumstances and fuel poverty, energy policy, energy supplies and the carbon and energy intensity of the economy, differences in circumstances between England, Scotland, Wales and Northern Ireland and circumstances at European and international level.

The Committee on Climate Change

The Government will also establish a Committee on Climate Change. The Committee will advise the Secretary of State on the level of the carbon budget for each five year period. The committee will also advise on the respective contributions towards meeting the budget that should be made by the sectors of the economy covered by trading schemes and the sectors that are not. Each year the Committee will report on progress towards meeting the carbon budget and the 2050 target.

Trading schemes

The Climate Change Bill permits the making of regulations to create a trading scheme for the purpose of limiting greenhouse gas emissions or encouraging activities that reduce such emissions or remove greenhouse gas from the atmosphere and to offer grants to the administrator of, or participants in, a trading scheme.

The regulations will identify the activities to which the scheme applies and the persons to whom it applies. The regulations may allocate allowances to permit participants in the scheme to carry on a specified amount of activities in a trading period. A participant who does not have enough allowances or credits might be allowed to pay to be authorised to trade during the trading period.

Impact of and adaptation to climate change

The Secretary of State must report to Parliament from time to time with an assessment of the risks for the UK of the current and predicted impact of climate change. The first report must be within three years of the Bill coming into force and each subsequent report no more than five years apart.

The Secretary of State must set out a programme showing the Government's objectives in relation to adaptation to climate change, proposals and policies for meeting those objectives and timescales for introducing those policies. The objectives, proposals and policies must contribute to sustainable development.

Climate change is firmly on the agenda

It is clear then that climate change is now firmly on the agenda. Regulation in this respect is likely to increase rather than decrease over time. Directors must stay up to date with the legal and regulatory changes that affect their business to ensure that they remain compliant at all times, and are able to predict the likely changes when forward planning for their business.

Director's legal responsibilities

The duties which apply to company directors are onerous and wide ranging. It is extremely important that directors understand what their duties are when making decisions on behalf of the company and what liability they potentially have if things go wrong.

Statutory general duties

Under the Companies Act 2006 directors have certain statutory general duties. These came into force on 1 October 2007.

The duty to exercise reasonable care, skill and diligence is also one that directors should be particularly aware of. In complying with this duty a director must exercise the care, skill and diligence that would be exercised by a reasonably diligent person with the general knowledge, skill and experience that may reasonably be expected of a person carrying out the functions carried out by the director and the general knowledge, skill and experience that the director actually has. Ignorance of the law is no defence and a director must therefore ensure that he has a level of awareness of the regulatory issues affecting his company in so far as that would reasonably be expected by someone in his position.

Limited liability

The principle of limited liability means that generally shareholders and directors are not liable for the acts or omissions of the company. This is because the company is regarded as a legal person in its own right separately from its shareholders and directors. However, this rule is subject to certain exceptions. A director may incur personal liability if he allows the company to do something which is outside the objects contained in its memorandum of association or which is illegal. He can also be personally liable if the company commits an offence under health and safety legislation with his consent or attributable to his neglect.

Generally, where companies commit environmental offences, prosecutions are brought against that company rather than any one individual who may have been responsible within the company. However, certain environmental statutes permit directors and managers to be prosecuted individually if the company commits an offence and there was consent, connivance or neglect by the individual concerned.

How to avoid prosecution

With the continual increase in regulation that businesses face it is ever more important to make sure that directors know what laws apply to the activities of their company, whether the business is compliant with these and if not, how to ensure compliance. Directors must make sure that the company obtains and complies with all necessary consents, licences and registrations and makes sure that all employees are aware of and comply with company policies.

Sarah Youren is a partner in the Planning and Environment team at Field Fisher Waterhouse. She advises on all aspects of planning and environmental law from inception to construction of a project. Her clients include private developers, funders, local authorities and Government organisations.

The Planning and Environment team advise on all aspects of planning and environmental law. We have a particular interest in sustainable development and help clients obtain planning permission, evaluate Environmental Impact Assessments, negotiate planning and infrastructure agreements and acquire sites through compulsory purchase. On the environmental side we offer skilled and commercial advice on issues such as flooding, contaminated land, waste, water pollution and recycling. We have considerable experience in the energy field and with flood related development.

Further details: www.ffw.com

6 Green taxes

"There are going to be tax advantages to going green", says Patrick King, Tax Principal at MacIntyre Hudson LLP.

There are no green taxes significant enough to prompt a small or medium-sized business to alter its tax planning. But this is about to change. Green taxes will undoubtedly become more stringent and wide ranging as the government struggles to meet its carbon reduction targets. Businesses should start planning now and ensure they take advantage of tax relief the government gives for green investments, and minimise exposure to new environmental taxes.

Reducing carbon emissions is now on the agenda of all the political parties. The Confederation of British Industry (CBI) has come out in strong support of the government's pledge to reduce carbon emissions. To achieve these goals, businesses of all shapes and sizes will be required to operate in an environmentally friendly fashion and produce green goods and services. Those that don't will be penalised, either through green taxation or through the higher cost of producing carbon emissions. Businesses must be 'green to grow', to coin the phrase of CBI Director General Richard Lambert.

As social awareness of climate change grows, businesses that fail to make their operations as energy efficient as possible will also lose the confidence of their customers. Companies in the FTSE100 and FTSE250 include environmental impact statements or 'triple bottom line reporting' in their financial results as a matter of course. This practice has not yet filtered down to SMEs but it is only a matter of time before they too are held to account.

On a positive note, there are substantial tax benefits for businesses making energy-saving investments that will reduce their tax bills in the short-term and their fuel and energy bills over the long-term.

Enhanced Capital Allowances for green investments

Businesses can take advantage of the Enhanced Capital Allowances (ECAs) on offer for energy-saving investments. All financial managers will be familiar with the tax allowances, called capital allowances, which can be claimed on certain purchases or investments. In effect, a proportion of these costs can be deducted from a business's taxable profits to reduce its tax bill. Capital allowances are available on plant and machinery, buildings (in limited circumstances, such as the converting of space above commercial premises to flats) and research and development.

The government has now introduced ECAs to encourage businesses to invest in energy-saving equipment, which is specified on the Energy Technology List (ETL), managed by the Carbon Trust, a government organisation that helps businesses and the public sector to cut carbon emissions.

The ECA scheme provides businesses with 100 per cent first year tax relief on their qualifying capital expenditure. This means businesses can write off the whole cost of the equipment against taxable profits in the year of purchase. It gives businesses a cash flow boost and acknowledges that energy-saving equipment often carries a price premium compared with less efficient alternatives. In contrast, the general rate of capital allowances for spending on plant and machinery for an SME is only 20 per cent a year.

For an SME paying corporation tax at 21 per cent (the new rate for small companies), every £1,000 spent on qualifying equipment would reduce its tax bill in the year of purchase by £210. In contrast, for every £1,000 spent, the generally available capital allowance of 20 per cent for spending on plant and machinery would reduce a business's tax bill in the year of purchase by only £42. In other words, an ECA could provide a cash flow boost of £168 for every £1,000 it spends in the year of purchase. For larger companies paying the higher rate of corporation tax, the maximum tax relief under ECA's increases to £280 per £1,000 with the cash flow boost compared to ordinary capital allowances being £238

Having said the above, the newly introduced 'annual investment allowance' of £50,000, which is for expenditure on most forms of plant and machinery, means that smaller company's will have no financial incentive to invest in green technologies. Expenditure within the annual allowance qualifies for 100% relief whether it is ECA type plant or not, such that the advantages mentioned above will only apply after the company has already made capital investments of over £50,000.

There are three schemes for ECAs. One covers energy-saving plant and machinery, the second covers low carbon dioxide emission cars and natural gas and hydrogen refuelling infrastructure, and the third covers water conservation plant and machinery. Between them, these schemes will cover most areas of a business's capital expenditure from lighting systems, to boilers and cars.

Just to give an example, since April 2002, ECAs have been available for new cars with carbon dioxide emissions of not more than 120gm per km driven for business use. These greener cars include the Toyota Prius, Honda Civic Hybrid, Ford Fusion and Renault Megane.

Recent research found that a fleet of 50 green cars would cost more up-front but would reap dramatic cost savings in the long-term. The average price of the 10 most fuel-efficient vehicles stands at £16,151 compared with £15,472 for the average price for the 10 most popular cars. However, when the reduced fuel and tax costs from the green fleet were taken into account, the study found that the higher initial start up costs would be recovered within 18 months. Furthermore, over a four-year period, the green fleet would cost almost £60,000 less compared with the conventional fleet and emit 134 tonnes less of carbon.

Given the apparent tax advantages, the take up of ECAs to date seems low. This may be explained by the level of persistence demanded of a business to identify which ECAs they are entitled to and then apply for them. In some situations, the ECA a business is entitled to may not be greater than an ordinary capital allowance. It is the upfront timing of the ECA that is advantageous.

Future tax incentives for businesses to go green

If the government is committed to reducing carbon emissions it needs to make energy efficient capital investments more economically attractive to businesses. A way to do this would be to increase the ECAs for certain equipment to 125 per cent. Alternatively, the government could increase VAT on polluting equipment, such as the 'dirty' boiler, water purification system or machinery.

Spiralling taxes on business travel

If there is one certainty, the cost of carbon is on an irreversible upward trajectory. With a 2p increase on excise duty on hydrocarbon fuels planned for the next two years, rising oil prices, and the doubling of air passenger duty, the economic argument for business travel is weakening.

To date, the tax hikes have not been substantial enough to significantly alter an SME's travel polices but it is enough to make them look for more low carbon alternatives. Investment in video conferencing will become a popular low-carbon and tax-avoidance alternative.

The Green Fiscal Commission, launched by the government in November 2007 to 'prepare the ground for a significant programme of green fiscal reform', is due to report in April 2009. It is envisaged it will recommend that 20 per cent of tax revenues come from green taxes by 2020. The commission is likely to focus on energy and transport as these are areas where large tax increases could be justified to reduce carbon emissions. By approaching capital investments from an environmental perspective, businesses can get ahead of the game, while benefiting from tax allowances, reducing their energy bills and enhancing their green credentials.

Patrick King is chairman of the firm's tax strategy group, leading a team of specialists which ensures clients have access to the very best in tax compliance services and tax mitigation solutions. Patrick's own specialisms are capital tax planning for individuals, corporate restructuring and remuneration planning. He also advises clients on the tax implications of buying and selling their business.

MacIntyre Hudson LLP is a top 25 UK accounting firm, offering a full range of compliance and advisory services to owner-managed businesses through to multinationals. The firm has 50 Principals and 380 staff situated in nine offices located across the Midlands, Home Counties and London. The firm is the UK member of CPA Associates International Inc with member firms worldwide, and is registered to carry on audit work and regulated for a range of business activities by The Institute of Chartered Accountants in England and Wales.

For more information contact: Patrick King, Tax Principal, MacIntyre Hudson LLP, patrick.king@mhllp.co.uk

Useful reference sites

The Carbon Trust www.thecarbontrust.co.uk

Energy Technology List www.eca.gov.uk/etl

Car Fuel Data www.vcacarfueldata.org.uk/

Part 2

Planning a response

7 Investment potential

Gareth Hughes, co-founder of Climate Change Capital, the investment banking group dedicated to a low carbon economy, gives his view on the role of private capital in combating climate change.

It is no exaggeration to say that our attempts to mitigate or adapt to climate change, while simultaneously addressing pressing energy security challenges, represent one of the greatest investment opportunities in history. Combating even the known rise in greenhouse gases will influence everything we manufacture and everything in which we invest, whether it be the obvious things like transport and energy production, or the not so obvious such as the design of new or retro-fitting of existing buildings so that they are 'clean and green', ie climate adapted. And it will not just affect those things we can feel and touch but also the very structure of some financial businesses, like those in insurance. Indeed, failure to have a properly constructed and accelerated process to reduce emissions could have significant unforeseen consequences for the stability of global financial markets and the future value of our investments.

This may sound as if I am in favour of making money from our fear about the future of the world, but I prefer to look at it another way. Combating climate change is certainly an economic opportunity as well as a necessity but it is also an example of how the use of private sector capital, through investment, can serve the common good. We like to call this creating 'wealth worth having'. There need be no trade-off between creating attractive returns and environmental integrity. In fact they are positively correlated.

CCC was founded four and half years ago with a simple mission to facilitate and accelerate the raising and deployment of capital at scale into the low carbon economy. We have built a bridge between the worlds of policy and finance, bringing a deep level of policy insight to the financial markets world and vice-versa.

We recognised too that climate change was a global problem which needs, in the main, a local and global response. After all there is only one atmosphere – whether you be in Manhattan or The Maldives. It is also worth pointing out that both these places, as different as they are, are at sea level.

At times on the CCC journey it has felt that we were, and are still at the cutting or indeed bleeding edge of emerging sustainable global and local environmental policy and regulation – working in the early stage of the development of new financial markets in carbon and clean technologies including waste and water. These markets have emerged out of a necessity to focus on the twin drivers of energy and environmental security. It took 100 years to build the existing energy infrastructure but we only have 100 months to transform how we produce, transmit and use energy and develop and implement the solutions, both policy and technology, to achieve the shift to a low carbon economy, stabilising global emissions and average temperature increase at 2-3 degrees – although some say it is already too late.

Needless to say, there is a pressing need to deploy capital quickly and at scale if we are going to avoid irreversible climate change and damage. The chaos in the financial system we have seen this spring will be nothing if these systems break down which they realistically could if anything other than the most conservative scientific predictions manifest themselves.

It is extraordinary that we have seen the creation of carbon as an asset class – the only one you cannot see. The Kyoto Protocol, a fascinating and absolutely necessary first step in creating global agreement, has created a nascent global carbon market based on the understanding that it doesn't matter where the carbon is taken out of the atmosphere. At the moment many of the deals to eliminate carbon have involved China. This will change and the higher price of carbon the more careful companies will have to become in their production of it. In effect Kyoto has kick started the process to find market based solutions to a collective problem.

In the carbon market, high energy consuming companies and carbon finance specialists from developed countries can invest in projects in developing countries which utilise low carbon technologies where the cost of emission reductions are lower. It has, together with more conventional investments, enabled the private sector to see the opportunity for making profit by allocating capital at scale into the developing world, thus enabling the transfer of technology to start the shift towards a global lower carbon objective.

Carbon will not be the last new asset class. I can see trees, so vital to ecosystems everywhere but still being cut down, becoming one. The question there is quite simple: How do you make a tree worth more alive than dead? The world needs to find a way of rewarding people to keep trees growing. Already in Africa there is a company, backed by CCC, called TIST, the International Small Group and Tree Planting Programme which is doing this in a small but constructive way. It expects to provide long-term revenue for the Small Group participants through the sale of greenhouse gas credits.

In India there are plans to have a whole district use low energy bulbs, so saving energy and making their erratic power supply more reliable but also producing carbon credits which will be sold to the developed world. The money to buy or subsidise the bulbs will come from companies like ours who will buy the credits and sell them.

But investment in the developing countries is one thing, what about nearer home? Everywhere people are thinking about how to make their companies and their homes more energy efficient, both to reduce carbon use and counter the soaring cost of energy. We at CCC have just appointed two experienced property investment managers to look at how commercial property can be made low carbon through change in both the design and operation of new and existing buildings. We see a growing market, with two tier pricing, in property with those buildings that are energy efficient and climate proofed being worth more than those that are not. Again, private money will be used and will produce profits and public good.

When we set up Climate Change Capital – the initial idea was crafted on the back of a napkin in the bar at a climate conference in Zurich – we realized there was no point in being too hair shirted about avoiding climate change. We need to reward innovation – learning and risk-taking in the search for emission reductions – and there will be losers as well as winners. But we need low carbon entrepreneurs all over the world looking to prosper by delivering the public good. We need a global forum or exchange for the proper development and funding of these ideas.

We also need to harness the mass mobilization of consumer purchasing power where consumers are rewarded for making informed decisions and getting low carbon choices when they buy everyday products. Financial institutions need to step up and promote loyalty and reward programmes that provide a rich and rewarding consumer experience with real and valuable knowledge sharing which will also drive beneficial behavioural change. We are involved with such an end-to-end solution.

The insurance market and institutional investors need to continue to take a leadership role in all aspects of climate change mitigation and adaptation. They need to move from strong dialogue and engagement with investee companies and policy-makers to making a significant allocation to those entities and investors who are committed to positive change and offer properly risk managed solutions, whether at the investment or product and service level. Companies whose business plans and risk management programmes clearly reflect environmental risks and opportunities should be rewarded. There is a natural hedge in such investments, and all existing and future investments need to consider the current and future cost of carbon and other environmental resources where the playing field has been truly leveled and the total and true cost of production analysed and assessed. Only then will there be a true climate for change.

Gareth Hughes is Managing Director and co-founder of Climate Change Capital, a leading investment banking group with over $1.5 billion under management that advises and invests in companies who recognise combating global warming is both a necessity and an economic opportunity. www.climatechangecapital.com

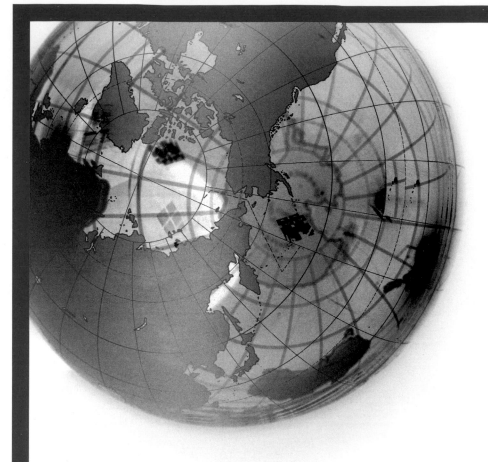

HSBC is actively involved in the following climate change
and sustainability leadership initiatives:

- HSBC Climate Partnership
- HSBC Climate Change Centre of Excellence
- The Bali Communiqué
- The Climate Group
- EPA Climate Leaders
- EPA Green Power Partners
- Equator Principles

- G8 Gleneagles Initiative
- CEO Roundtable on Climate Change
- Institutional Investors Group on Climate Change
- Principles for Responsible Investment
- Roundtable on Sustainable Palm Oil
- UNEP-Finance Initiative

Sunny Sehgal
Head of Environmental and Strategic Risk Consulting
HSBC Insurance Brokers
Tel: +44 (0) 20 7661 2331
Email: sunnysehgal@hsbc.com
Web: www.insurancebrokers.hsbc.com

Climate Change: risk or opportunity?

At HSBC, we understand the growing significance of climate change to our clients' businesses, in respect of both risk and opportunity.

The Climate Risk and Opportunity Review is a strategic risk consulting service that harnesses our immense climate change expertise.

Let us help you manage the risks and capture the opportunities from climate change.

HSBC Insurance

Issued by HSBC Insurance Brokers Limited.
HSBC Insurance Brokers Limited is a Lloyd's broker and is authorised and regulated by the Financial Services Authority, Firm reference number 310240.

8 Enterprise risk

"Climate change is starting to affect enterprises at a strategic level. There are bound to be winners and losers", says Sunny Sehgal at HSBC Insurance Brokers, "so early high-level review is essential."

What has emerged over the last few years is agreement that climate change is affecting or will affect a wide range of industry sectors, some more than others, and that there are both risks and opportunities to be endured or exploited.

Figure 1 shows a simplistic representation of how certain industry sectors are likely to fare at a macro-level, in terms of being winners or losers, out of climate change.

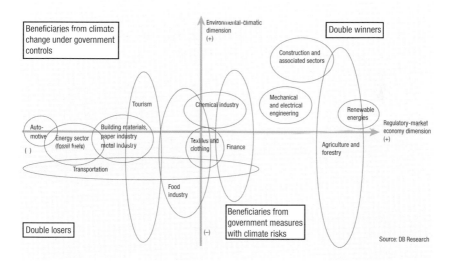

Figure 1: Winning and Losing Sectors from Climate Change
(Reference: Climate Change and Sectors: Some like it hot!, DB Research, July 2007)

Notes to Figure 1:

- The horizontal axis indicates benefits from governmental actions to tackle climate change through regulatory (e.g. legislation) tools and market-based tools (e.g. taxes), with those on the right hand side being 'winners' and those on the left being 'losers'. An example of such regulatory action is the Kyoto Protocol aimed at reducing carbon emissions. The axis could equally represent relative benefits from the drive towards a lower carbon economy – the CARBON axis or dimension.

- The vertical axis indicates impacts from physical climate change impacts (ie the IMPACTS axis or dimension), with those on the upper section being 'winners' and those on the lower section being 'losers'. Examples of a physical climate change impact is rising sea-levels and drought.

- The sizes of the circles and ellipses reflect the extent to which those industry sectors are affected rather than their size or importance.

The graph is a striking visual representation of:

i)   the broad range of industry sectors that are being or will be affected by climate change (the timeframe given is from a few years to two decades);

ii) from a business perspective, the considerable up-side (opportunity) as well as the more familiar down-side (risk) context in which climate change is normally considered.

Given its global significance, many studies on climate change, whether in terms of CARBON or IMPACTS, look at long-term horizons, typically >10 years. This may, unintentionally, create a sense of comfort to all but the largest enterprises that this is 'tomorrow's problem' and that there are many other pressing matters to be dealt with in the here and now. However, there is good reason to think that pro-active rather than reactive responses to climate change will be a feature of tomorrow's successful enterprises. In particular, there are both clear and subtle signs that climate change is effecting enterprises today.

Risks and opportunities are clearly starting to materialise along the carbon dimension. The traditionally carbon intensive sectors, such as automotive, fossil fuel energy and manufacturing are starting to see a compromise in a 'business as usual' approach in light of the drive towards low carbon. Hence such industries congregate on the left part of the carbon axis in Figure 1. Note that carbon emission reduction targets starting to affect the automotive sector and also European Union Emissions Trading Scheme (EU ETS) which include the energy intensive industries. While such measures may not be material to their survival currently, it should be expected that regulators, shareholders and society at large will only increase the pressure towards low carbon business. The materiality of climate risk is therefore likely to increase in the near future.

Conversely, renewable energy technologies are and will continue to benefit from increased governmental assistance (e.g. UK Renewable Obligation Certificates) and are therefore represented on the right side of the carbon axis. Note the various targets being set, particularly within Europe, around contributions to power generation from renewable energy sources, such as wind, solar, biomass etc. and the associated investment activity in low carbon technologies or so-called 'Cleantech'.

However, there are other less obvious trends starting to emerge and affect a wider range of industry sectors in the IMPACTS dimension, some of these are described below:

Tourism will no doubt continue to be a growth sector, but clearly needs to be mindful of the impacts dimension of climate change. Warmer winter temperatures may mean shorter snow seasons and a reduction in snow cover with impacts to ski resorts, but perhaps greater 'winter sun' opportunities for some locations; higher summer temperatures could effect the timing and destination of bookings (due to excess heat) and lead to fire / health impacts; increased coastal flooding, the strain on natural resources (e.g. freshwater) and ecological systems ('eco-tourism') from climate change may also affect the tourism sector in both extreme and subtle ways. Some regions will benefit from climate change whereas others will face threats. In respect of the carbon dimension, a more significant carbon cost is likely to be imposed on air travel, thereby potentially rendering long-haul tourism more expensive.

Agriculture and forestry sectors are likely to benefit in the carbon dimension of climate risk from an increased long-term demand for biofuels, such as maize, sugar beet and wood fuels, to replace fossil fuels. Also there is significant potential for the sector to help assist in the sequestration (capturing) of atmospheric carbon in forests and managed biomass. However, 'food versus fuel' conflicts have already started to emerge, with noticeable global price effects in recent years on agricultural products.

The changes in climatic and weather patterns (the impacts dimension of climate risk) could bring benefits to some areas, including northern latitudes, through improving soil conditions but also severe threats to other areas prone to drought (e.g. southern Europe) and more extreme weather events such as hurricanes and hailstorms.

Finance sectors including insurance, banking and investment also need to consider at a strategic level the brand, operational, credit, underwriting and investment risks arising out of both dimensions of climate change. Insurance is particularly vulnerable to the impacts dimension of climate risk through its exposures to major property and human impacts from extreme weather events.

As with other sectors, the most forward thinking financial institutions will be the ones most likely to benefit from climate risk – namely once their own risks have been identified and managed, then there is considerable potential to innovate and offer products and services around the climate change agenda. 'Green' banking, investment and (more recently) insurance products have been in existence for some years now to capitalise upon the carbon dimension of climate risk. Existing financial products that inherently protect against weather and climatic uncertainty (e.g. flood insurance, weather derivatives etc.) are also now being re-packaged and tailored to harness the impacts dimension of climate risk.

Construction, engineering and other associated sectors are likely to benefit in several ways from climate risk. Under the carbon dimension, buildings account for around 50% of carbon emissions from man-made sources, and there is a considerable scope for buildings to be made more energy efficient, resulting also in lower fuel bills. Refurbishing existing building stock and improving the energy efficiency of new buildings through innovation will be features of 'quick-win' strategies for reducing carbon emissions from both public and private building stock.

Significant capital investment will also need to be made in respect of the impacts dimension of climate risk, whether as precautionary (e.g. construction and improvement of coastal defences in vulnerable locations) or reactive measures (repair of damage to property and infrastructure from extreme weather events such as Hurricane Katrina). In both cases, the construction, engineering and associated industries can expect more significant contracts as a result of climate risk.

Developing your own perspective on climate change

Given the far-reaching and inter-related implications of climate change, it is difficult for senior management of any given enterprise to understand immediately how best to consider the full implications to their enterprise. For example, our research indicates that very few enterprises would be able to robustly answer the following questions:

- Where would your enterprise currently be positioned on the graph in Figure 1 and why?

- How can your enterprise minimise the risks and maximise the benefits from climate change to gain advantage over competitors?

- Does your enterprise have a governance requirement to identify, evaluate and control climate risk?

Furthermore, for enterprises of all sizes, there can be confusion as to which area, department or individual should be charged with managing climate risk. The following are just some of the areas of an enterprise that may need to consider and take responsibility for climate change matters to a greater or lesser extent (listed in no particular order nor priority):

- Risk management and insurance (physical hazards and liability)

- PR/communications (corporate social responsibility, brand)

- Finance (climate risk financing issues, including carbon trading, pension investments)

- Governance and corporate reporting

- Facilities management, IT and corporate real estate (energy use, own carbon footprint)

- Health, safety and environment, HSE (process and compliance)

- Procurement and travel (carbon usage in supply chain, employees' business travel)

- Product development (climate change related products)

- Legal (contractual matters)

- Human resources (people increasingly want to work for 'green' companies).

There are further layers of complexity in respect of different geographical territories, corporate finance structure (parents and subsidiaries), corporate finance transactions (mergers and acquisitions) and outsourcing of responsibilities. Also note that trusted professional advisors such as lawyers, accountants, architects and engineers may also have undeveloped or unaligned perspectives on climate change.

Addressing these questions and uncertainties has to begin with your enterprise developing its own perspective on climate change. This is achieved through undertaking a high level Climate Risk and Opportunity Review.

Climate Risk and Opportunity Review (CROR)

At HSBC, we recommend undertaking a Climate Risk and Opportunity Review (CROR) to start the process of addressing climate change. In designing CROR for any given enterprise, we can employ some valuable techniques from Enterprise Risk Management (ERM) (see Box 1).

The scope, process and output of CROR, as with ERM, should be tailored to the specific enterprise, and can be as simple as a single workshop involving senior management through to a longer term risk management programme, involving all levels of the enterprise. Objectivity is important and therefore the process is best facilitated by an external expert in Climate Risk and should have senior management backing.

The CROR aims to recognise and prioritise all climate risks and opportunities that may face the enterprise – the main output from the CROR is a 'map' of key or 'primary' risks and opportunities, showing also their interrelationship and corresponding impacts – or 'secondary' risks and opportunities. The output of the CROR is then integrated, using an ERM approach, into the enterprise's processes, risk financing and capital allocation relating to risk management and opportunity capturing.

The following are example CROR maps for enterprises involved in three of the sectors described in the previous section showing some typical primary risks and opportunities only (with red text showing risks and green text showing opportunities).

Tourism company

ERM risk / opportunity	Carbon dimension	Impacts dimension
Financial		Downturn in demand caused by unexpected weather leading to cashflow risk
Operational		Increased health impacts e.g. malaria
Strategic	Future cost of flying / mobility (carbon cost) Carbon off-setting, 'green' branding	Warmer winters affecting ski resorts Winter sun resorts
Hazard		

Insurance company

ERM risk / opportunity	Carbon dimension	Impacts dimension
Financial		Exposure to natural catastrophe underwriting risk in climate vulnerable locations
Operational		Increased health impacts e.g. malaria
Strategic	Green, climate-friendly products e.g. pay as you go motor, insurance for renewables Green branding	Climate-proof products e.g, flood insurance, weather derivatives
Hazard		Director's and Officer's – overexposure to natural catastrophe

Engineering company

ERM risk / opportunity	Carbon dimension	Impacts dimension
Financial		
Operational	Training of employees in respect of energy design	
Strategic	Energy and carbon emissions regulation	
Hazard	Professional Liability Insurance – energy design advice	

Conclusion

There is a growing need for enterprises of all sizes to develop their own perspective on climate risk. A Climate Risk and Opportunity Review (CROR) should be the foundation of your enterprise's strategy towards successfully managing the risks and capturing the opportunities out of climate change.

Enterprise Risk Management (ERM)

ERM is a methodology of identifying, quantifying and prioritising a wide range of risks and recognising that they may correlate, rather than just focusing on silos of individual risks. The need for an increased awareness of risk that has made ERM grow in prominence in recent times, further driven by regulatory demand and the perception of a riskier business environment. It is a versatile concept that can span all enterprises of all sizes.

The following table outlines the four categories of risks that fall within the scope of ERM:

ERM RISK (& OPPORTUNITY)	DESCRIPTION	EXAMPLE RISK TYPES
Financial risk	Risks that relate to treasury and investment activities of the Operation	Commodity Liquidity Counterparty Credit Equity portfolio fluctuations
Operational risk	Risks that relate to the people, processes and technologies necessary to produce and sell an Operation's products	Financial reporting Environmental compliance Manufacturing quality control Supply chain interruption Fund transfer controls System continuity Human error Information Technology
Strategic risk	Risks relating to the Operation's decision-making process at the senior management and board level	Product obsolescence Competition Industry over capacity Reputation Brand erosion Law and regulation Capital availability
Hazard risk	Unforeseen events that arise outside the normal operating environment of the Operation (often insurable)	Employers' liability Directors' and Officers' liability Property damage Terrorism Product liability Weather perils Business interruption

Table 1: Enterprise Risk Management

HSBC Insurance Brokers is one of the largest international insurance broking, risk management and employee benefits organisations in the world.

We have the depth of knowledge to analyse complex risk situations from multiple perspectives and develop comprehensive solutions that meet the specific needs of our clients. We are the only major insurance broker that forms part of a global banking group. As members of the HSBC Group we share an international network with offices in countries and territories in Europe, the Asia-Pacific region, the Americas, the Middle East and Africa.

Based in London, Sunny Sehgal heads the Environmental and Strategic Risk Consulting Practices of HSBC Insurance Brokers. As a former consultant, Sunny has worked with a wide range of clients in managing environmental risk. His role within HSBC involves creating innovative advisory and insurance solutions for environmental, climate change and sustainability risks. Sunny is also a Member of the United Nations Environment Programme (UNEP FI) Insurance Working Group.

Further details: Sunny Sehgal, Head of Environmental and Strategic Risk Consulting, HSBC Insurance Brokers Tel: +44 (0) 20 7661 2331 Email: sunnysehgal@hsbc.com Web: www.insurancebrokers.hsbc.com

Arthur D Little

Realising the Carbon Margin

The Global Carbon Advisory Team

How businesses respond to the carbon agenda is complex. Yet, a correctly positioned carbon strategy can allow companies to outperform their competitors by as much as 20% — it makes sense to get it right.

Arthur D. Little's GCAS team supports businesses by translating economic, environmental and policy drivers for carbon into strategies that makes business sense.

The creation of the GCAS team adds to the leading edge capabilities of Arthur D. Little's Global Practices.

To find out how we can help your company realise its carbon advantage call us on 0845 3366716 or visit our website www.adl.com for more information and case studies.

www.adl.com/gcas

9 Rethinking carbon

"Carbon is rewriting the rules of competition in business",
say David Lyon and Melissa Barrett, Global Carbon Advisory
Services, Arthur D. Little.

Business, politics, academia and consumers across the globe are increasingly concerned about the impact of greenhouse gas emissions on the health, prosperity and future of society. Media reports focus attention on natural or economic disasters related to climate change. Politicians consider the restrictions and constraints on how businesses operate, and how people live, in order to reduce emissions and hence combat climate change.

In recent years, governments have issued a plethora of new emissions-curbing regulations and targets: e.g. in US states such as California, spurring action more recently at Federal level; the UK's draft Climate Change Bill; the EU's target to cut CO_2 emissions by 20% by the year 2020; and others. These can have a significant impact on the way (particularly multinational) businesses plan and manage their facilities, vehicle fleets and supply chains. Naturally, the energy intensive sectors are among the first to have to develop the competencies to respond to drivers such as cap and trade mechanisms, national regulation, and supply chain pressures.

The impact of 'carbon' on the globalization of business can be seen most readily, perhaps, by considering countries like China or India. As the recent United Nations Global Environmental Outlook pointed out, these rapidly emerging economies are extremely vulnerable to the impact of rising greenhouse gas emissions. They are also prime opportunity spaces for companies seeking to expand through globalization – even more so if such companies can offer products and/or services that will help to address causes and sources of climate change.

Meanwhile, 'carbon' is helping to rewrite the rules of competition in business. Companies that are seen to respond better to the needs of their stakeholders – e.g. consumers seeking 'greener' products or investors requiring improved risk management can gain competitive advantage in many forms. These include improved reputation, improved sales, and improved access to talent, capital and resources. As the Arthur D. Little/ECPI Carbon Winners Index listed on Bloomberg shows, companies with better current and future carbon management strategies outperform their peers by as much as 20%.

Arthur D. Little has coined the term 'carbon margin' pointing to the new profit margins to be made or retained by companies that manage their carbon exposure well: not just making savings through energy efficiencies, avoiding environmental taxes and the like, but creating new revenue streams and even new businesses related to the carbon debate. These opportunities are driven by clean-technologies, developing new business models and exploiting future carbon markets.

The carbon margin can be defined as the Top Line (opportunities, choices, and revenues) minus the Bottom Line (costs). Considering carbon within corporate strategies creates more options for the business: new product ideas emerge; new markets become viable; people find new ways of working and forge innovative partnerships.

By recognising and addressing the climate change concerns of its stakeholders, a company is better able to manage risks to its reputation, customer and supplier base, employee and recruitment pool, business operations and financial performance. Moreover, a company's proficiency at managing the risks related to climate change is increasingly seen among financial institutions as an important indicator of its overall management capability, which in turn strongly affects the ability to raise finance.

A true carbon margin relies on harnessing these opportunities and using best practice in managing carbon exposure today to realise profit margins tomorrow.

Source of opportunities

Companies seeking to grasp carbon opportunities that are not yet formed will need new strategies, new technologies and new ways of working.

Creating a carbon-integrated strategy

To create a carbon-integrated company strategy, carbon management needs to be represented at board level, not by an 'add-on' group or executive. Clarity is required around the reasons for the new strategy so that cost-cutting and emission reduction does not automatically take precedence over efforts to create new low-carbon businesses. How the company measures its performance must be transparent to all; the most common ground tends to be around energy efficiency, although this often only benefits emissions reduction when energy prices are high.

Many external issues feed into developing a carbon-integrated strategy. Companies can not rely on mapping out the marginal abatement costs of alternative measures or technologies alone. Rather, companies need to develop a strategy that incorporates key enabling factors including:

1. developing a process to map out future standards and regulatory alternatives;

2. mapping out influences of inequalities in the value chain (regarding the costs of CO_2 mitigation and how they can be passed on to other players); and

3. forecasting which technologies will actually be available and commercially viable at defined points in the future.

To deal with such complexity, companies need strategies that can respond to a range of probable scenarios, rather than a single set of forecasts or predictions. For example, Arthur D. Little developed a suite of scenarios for the automotive industry based on key drivers such as oil price, regulation and consumer behaviour. These scenarios indicate the different opportunities for car makers to expand the global market for existing classes of cars and developing new areas of business (e.g. assisting consumers to reduce CO_2 emissions following vehicle sales, use of green-labelling).

Exploiting low-carbon technologies

Companies need a sound understanding of the likely changes in supply and demand for carbon abatement. Low-carbon technologies offer major opportunities for companies pursuing carbon-integrated strategies. However, both users and developers of such technologies face an array of complex options and influences. Good decision-making will require an informed and balanced view of all sides of the current debates. For example, cost estimates presented in various reports, commentaries and discussions are underpinned by assumptions (not always evident from the headline figures) that include capital costs, discount rates, economic life, input fuel costs and cost of carbon. These vary from study to study, materially affect the final values and so add to the complexity of choosing technologies to suit.

The most robust technology choices bring together insights from several different industries, and take into account their interrelationships and interdependencies. For example, Arthur D. Little has used a multidimensional approach to support a major European oil company looking to identify areas at which the company could successfully integrate carbon capture and storage (CCS) into its value chain.

Once companies have developed a robust understanding of low-carbon technologies they need to consider the most appropriate approach to exploit the opportunities. For example, a chemicals company were looking to draw on their existing competencies to exploit future sustainable energy markets such as distributed generation. With support from Arthur D. Little, the company identified future low-carbon markets, developed a platform bringing together internal and external competencies, a technology development process and an understanding of future markets.

Developing new ways of working to respond to a low-carbon economy

One of the most powerful ways of working to identify opportunities around carbon and climate change is based on systems thinking. These approaches help companies go beyond measurements of performance to understand the underlying dynamics causing it. Companies need to respond to markets as they evolve, and consider how to translate their targets into action. This could be through key dynamics such as carbon tax, and cap and trade mechanisms as well as offsetting mechanisms such as CDM.

There are numerous examples of companies using climate change to develop radical innovation. In our experience with utilities, profit margins can be doubled through initiating new low-carbon business streams. In intelligent transport systems, mobile phone companies, public transport providers, insurers, governments and others work together to develop solutions to reduce fuel consumption, vehicle wear and transportation times as well as integrate different modes of transportation. These examples illustrate the importance of using ideas of open innovation where suppliers, universities, customers all play a key role in helping companies respond to and develop a low-carbon economy.

Best practice today underpins future success

Any company's potential to grasp tomorrow's carbon and climate change opportunities depends, at least partly, on how well it manages its carbon exposure today. Benchmarking exercises carried out by Arthur D. Little in all major sectors show that today's leaders at managing their carbon exposure share some common ground. Not least, they demonstrate best practice by taking a holistic approach: defining a positioning and strategy that satisfies their stakeholders; developing the necessary processes; and aligning their organization and resources appropriately.

In the top quartile companies, carbon strategy is seen to be shaped by internal and external expertise, with scheduled reviews built into the design. The strategy is led by senior management and set by a diverse team including leadership from board level and all levels of management and employees. Once set, the strategy is clearly expressed, ideally by the CEO. In setting the strategy, the company includes a baseline assessment to accommodate major changes.

How carbon management fits within the overall organization of a company has a significant effect on the company's benchmarking results. In many companies, carbon management has been allocated to the External Affairs or the Environment, Health and Safety department. Better organized companies may still have division of labour – a corporate sustainability group making sure the company's emissions efforts are progressing, and a technology group providing the means to maintain the effort – but the whole is under the careful supervision of the company leadership team, because carbon management is seen (rightly) as a whole-business issue.

The processes that will most influence the desired outcomes can be identified from a company's strategic positioning:

1. in terms of how proactive or reactive it intends to be relative to legislation and consumers; and

2. how much it intends to push low-carbon technologies or be pulled by low-carbon market forces.

For example, a technology-intensive company is likely to focus on honing its R&D processes; a company at the other end of the technology focus scale may concentrate more on its marketing or distribution processes. Correct positioning requires companies to track and respond to new regulations regarding carbon markets. Energy-intensive companies (especially in Europe) are responding to increasing carbon prices under future emissions trading schemes – e.g. for one pan-European company, Arthur D. Little set up processes that enable the organization to trade carbon credits within and between its operations, across borders.

Monitoring and measuring new or improved processes is vital. Overall, best practice today includes clear monitoring and reporting that allows for comparison across years and sections of the company. Full public disclosure often follows guidelines such as the Global Reporting Initiative (GRI), United Nations Global Compact, and the Carbon Disclosure Project (CDP) among others.

Finally, among the resources evident in best-practice companies is a well honed skill set with the capability to know when to trust an opportunity, e.g. for carbon funds, carbon emissions offsetting or low-carbon technology investment. Where this capability is properly integrated with the unique combination of other competences in the organization, the impact on current operations and opportunities to create a platform for sustainable innovation and business creation in the future are unparalleled.

David Lyon is a Manager in Arthur D. Little's Sustainability and Risk Practice. David has ten years experience in advising governments and the private sector on sustainable and low carbon development, technology and innovation, business planning, socio-economic impact assessments, and public policy analysis. David is a senior member of Arthur D. Little's GCAS team. David Lyon +44 8703366754 lyon.david@adlittle.com

Melissa Barrett is a Consultant in Arthur D. Little's Sustainability and Risk Practice. Melissa has ten years experience in the environmental field with a focus on water and low carbon issues across businesses, government departments and for biodiversity. Melissa is a member of Arthur D. Little's GCAS team. Melissa Barrett +44 8703366774 barrett.melissa@adlittle.com

Arthur D. Little's GCAS team helps manage the complexity and confusion surrounding carbon management debates driven by policy, consumers, supply chain etc for both companies and investors by providing solutions that embrace the complexity and unlock value. http://www.adl.com/gcas

10 Climate change: the starting point

"Even multinationals struggle to be sure of where they stand on climate change and where they want to be in two years", says Tom Woollard of ERM.

Multinational companies frequently have no idea where to start when it comes to responding to the climate change agenda. How do we calculate the company's carbon footprint? How do we set energy reduction targets? How do we offset the company's direct impacts? These are all questions which can create confusion and sometimes paralysis around the climate change issue.

Given all the publicity on climate change, especially in Europe, many companies want to be able to tell the outside world what they are doing, rather than wait 2-3 years so that they can show demonstrable improvement in their performance. Despite the fact that annual energy performance improvements against stringent, internally set reduction targets are probably the most important contribution a company can make; they are much less exciting and have not caught the public's imagination in the same way that generating new 'low carbon products' or 'going carbon neutral' has.

Only a handful of the top FTSE 50 companies have a dedicated climate change manager to identify the main priorities and initiate a corporate-wide management program. In most companies the initial response to the climate change agenda usually falls to a combination of the strategy department, the risk manager, the environmental, health and safety team and corporate affairs – often leading to a significant amount of inertia in the early stages. The climate change strategy will vary in content and scope according to industry and company specific pressures, concerns and opportunities as well as what management, technical and financial resources are in place to manage the relevant issues. To some extent the climate change strategy will also be dependent upon the corporate departments (and lead department) brought in to develop the strategy. Getting the balance right between outward and inward facing programs; product can be is fraught with difficulty.

How does climate change affect business directly?

Climate change has become a mainstream story that impacts on businesses ranging from heavy manufacturing to logistics and retail. Not surprisingly, the story crops up in global media on a daily basis and, as such, it can be used to highlight shortcomings that could affect your company's reputation or conversely be used to generate competitive advantage through profile raising. There are a number of ways in which business will be directly affected by climate change, not least:

- **Customers**: the perception that consumers will increasingly shun products and brands that are linked to 'the problem';

- **Direct impacts**: increased threat from more severe weather extremes in the short-term and more gradual temperature and sea level fluctuations in the longer term;

- **Energy concerns**: fluctuations in oil prices and concerns about security combined with the rapid growth in clean alternative energy technologies (currently wind and solar investment is growing at more than 50% per annum) pose critical short and long-term dilemmas for large energy intensive industries;

- **Financial interest**: investors are seeking greater disclosure from companies of their climate change-related risks and opportunities (e.g. Company Law Reform 2006 and The Walker Report 2007), and are likely to value companies that are prepared for climate change higher than those that are not.

Getting started with self-assessment tools

At the initial stage of formulating a climate change strategy, once the pressures and opportunities have been clearly mapped out, companies may want to use one of a number of different tools to help determine the most effective strategy. Management tools that are typically used at this stage may include the faithful SWOT analysis (an assessment of strengths, weaknesses, opportunities, threats), benchmarking (usually against peer companies), regulatory and trend analysis (also known as 'horizon scanning' to assess existing and forthcoming pressure) and SCAN diagnostic (a form of gap analysis against the range of options available). Whilst there is a lot of information on the first three of these techniques, much less has been written on the use of gap analyses to determine climate change strategies.

The SCAN (Strategic Corporate Assessment of Needs) diagnostic tool enables senior management to assess where they are, where they would like to be within 2-3 years and how they propose to get there. It is easy to run and allows non-specialists to articulate their company's climate change priorities and where to focus limited resources. Whilst the SCAN tool can be run 'in-house', it is often a good idea to get a climate change specialist to facilitate this process. Essentially the SCAN diagnostic approach involves running a half or one day workshop for 6-12 senior managers asking them to informally score their company's performance in a number of areas.

The elements that are typically scored in a climate change SCAN diagnostic include:

- Strategy and targets
- GHG inventory and carbon footprint
- Measurement and reporting
- Impact/risk models
- Governance
- Regulatory tracking
- External communications disclosure
- Employee programmes
- Energy use
- Capital programmes
- Carbon trading and offset
- Process mapping
- Customer and product programmes
- Supplier programmes

The participants are asked to collectively select and agree on one of five graduated statements (from little or no activity to 'best in class' activity) that most clearly represent the company's current state of play. So, for example, on 'energy use' and 'supplier programmes' the five responses for each element may be as follows:

Energy use

- We track our energy consumption at site or unit level.

- We have undertaken an energy audit and have conducted energy awareness campaigns. We have a group-wide purchasing strategy that takes climate change into account.

- We have developed energy reduction KPIs and have set targets. We have resources and budgets in place to deliver and report on progress.

- We are making significant headway on energy reduction and have replaced the majority of inefficient equipment.

- Our targets are stretch targets (+/- 25% reduction), not bottom up targets, and hence force 'breakthrough' thinking into the organisation.

Supplier programmes

- We are waiting for industry-wide initiatives to share the cost of engaging suppliers.

- Purchasing department training is underway.

- We have an auditing programme in place to develop carbon footprints for all our products, including all suppliers, materials, packaging and transport.

- We are redesigning the supply chain and starting to examine the tradeoffs between stock levels, load factors and delivery frequencies in the context of climate change.

- Supplier's carbon footprint is an essential component of our supplier selection process. We view climate change as a way to advance our existing best practice work with suppliers. We have focused on joint innovation with our suppliers to deliver higher levels of energy and emissions savings.

Once all the elements have been scored, the group of senior managers are then asked to look forward over 2-3 years. In doing so the senior managers are asked to take into consideration forthcoming pressure from regulators, customers and competitors, any potential impacts from future mergers and acquisitions, any new product and/or company-wide developments and any potential opportunities in commercial, financial or political arenas. The group is then asked to review the same list of elements and scoring criteria and agree where the company should be aiming to get to in 2-3 years time. The resulting analysis between 'where we are now' and 'where we would like to be' provides a useful means of identifying the biggest gaps and where the company's climate change priorities may lie (see diagram below).

Area / Issue		Score				
		1	2	3	4	5
A	Measurement & Reporting	●			X	
B	GHG Inventory / Carbon Footprint		● ➡	X		
C	Governance			●X		
D	Strategy & Targets			●	X	
E	Energy Use			● ➡X		
F	Regulation Watch		●	X		
G	Impact / Risk Models	●				X
H	Carbon Trading & Offset / Reduction Balance		● ➡	X		
I	Process Mapping	●			X	
J	Employee Programmes / Awareness				●X	
K	Customer & Product Programmes		● ➡	X		
L	Supplier Programmes		● ➡	X		
M	Capital Programmes			● ➡	X	
N	External Communications & Disclosure			● ➡X		

Figure 1: ERM diagnostic for assessing climate change priorities

For the larger gaps, 'business as usual' is unlikely to close the gap and therefore new programs and initiatives are likely to be required. It is important to bear in mind that the priorities are not necessarily those elements with the largest gaps. Given the nature of the company's business, what competitors are doing and what pressure is being brought to bear on the company, decisions need to be made as to where best to invest the company's resources. The prioritisation process is essential as most companies have only limited time, money, and expertise to deal with these issues and clearly can't do everything at once.

Clearly the advantage of this approach is that it raises the general levels of awareness of the implications of climate change for a company as well as enabling the senior management team to review the range of options available to them and collectively work on a strategy. To achieve best results the process does need facilitation by someone who understands what climate change options are available and where the biggest short, medium and long-term gains can be achieved.

Spending appropriate time and resources defining a clear climate change strategy is essential and will help to save money and management effort in the short, medium and long-term. If implemented effectively and efficiently the strategy will also help to prevent costly, reactive and 'knee-jerk' responses to climate change pressures that arise in the future.

ERM's climate change and risk teams offer services to help clients answer the following questions:

- How will climate change impact my businesses?

- What are the key climate change threats?

- Where are the greatest climate change impacts?

- What is the likely magnitude of impact?

- What climate change mitigation and adaptation options should be considered?

Tom Woollard is a Principal Partner and member of the executive committe at ERM UK. Tom has been advising multinational corporations on a wide range of environmental and sustainability issues for the last 20 years.

Further details: www.erm.com

11 Energy efficiency

If you are serious about cutting your use of energy, then there are three steps that you have to take according to EDF Energy.

Not forgetting rising energy costs, growing political and consumer concerns around climate change are compelling companies to adopt a more sustainable approach to managing their activities. At EDF Energy, we believe sustainability plans should begin with energy efficiency as this can rapidly deliver carbon savings and quantifiable financial rewards too. In fact energy efficiency is becoming a more important component of sustainability action plans as it appears that new legislation (see below) will no longer recognise the purchasing of renewable energy as a carbon saving activity. For those preparing to take action to cut their energy use, these are some key issues to consider.

Three key drivers for energy efficiency

A previously neglected activity, there are three principle reasons for the resurgence of interest in energy efficiency in industry:

1. Costs

Energy costs are significantly higher today than they were three to four years ago. This has come as quite a shock for many, for at least a decade preceding 2003, energy costs had followed a comfortable downward trend in real terms. But having reaped the early benefits of deregulation and competition in all aspects of the UK's energy markets, we have to accept that the future will be less comfortable. We now face a climate of higher energy costs due to a wide range of factors including soaring global energy demand, new environmental legislation, and the need for investment in the UK's energy infrastructure to meet our future energy needs. But every cloud has its silver lining and in this case it's a stronger argument for investing in being more energy efficient – the financial returns are greater than ever.

2. Climate change

Climate change is on everyone's lips these days. Taking action to substantially reduce our carbon emissions is important for our future prosperity. The economic costs (never mind the social and environmental costs) of global temperatures rising much higher than 2 degrees above pre-industrial levels will be unpalatably high – from 5 to 20 per cent of global GDP according to the Stern Report. Unfortunately we're nearing the half way mark of that limit as temperatures rose by three quarters of a degree in the last century. So businesses need to act with a sense of urgency to reduce their carbon emissions. Retailers have been particularly vocal about their plans to cut carbon from their business operations – reflecting the risks to brands of savvy consumers shunning high carbon businesses. Energy use is a major source of carbon emissions and improvements in energy efficiency deliver immediate and lasting carbon cuts. They can be substantial too – often delivering around 10 to 20 per cent reductions with little investment.

3. Legislation

The case for tackling energy efficiency will continue to grow stronger through new legislation too. The Government is implementing a new scheme, called the Carbon Reduction Commitment (CRC), to help reduce carbon emissions in a wide range of business and public sector organisations. Around 5,000 organisations that spend more than £500,000 a year on electricity will qualify. They will then be part of a mandatory emissions trading scheme which will limit the overall carbon dioxide emissions caused by energy use – which contribute almost 10 per cent of the entire UK economy's emissions. The scheme will be an important part of the national effort to reduce the UK's total carbon footprint, and will save at least 4 million tonnes of carbon dioxide per year by 2020. Although all the details of the scheme are not 100% finalised, it appears that the scheme will no longer allow firms to claim carbon emissions savings based simply on purchasing renewable energy from energy suppliers. Energy efficiency therefore, looks to be the most effective strategy to follow for the foreseeable future.

Taking positive action

Yet, despite more attractive payback periods and the mitigating effect on brand risk, many businesses still struggle to implement energy efficiency initiatives. So, at EDF Energy we've developed practical ways to help businesses overcome the barriers they face.

Energy efficiency for large energy users

The potential for increasing energy efficiency in industry is significant and good progress has been made, particularly by energy intensive industries. The steel industry for example has more than halved the amount of energy used to produce a ton of steel since the '70s. But there remains enormous scope for further improvements as technologies keep advancing. With average annual equipment renewal rates of 5-6 per cent, industry is well placed to invest in more energy efficient equipment and practices, and see good returns.

In recent years EDF Group has worked with companies in France and Germany to deliver commercially rewarding energy saving activities through our Advanced Efficiency Programmes – a service bringing the expertise of our energy R&D facilities to businesses using large amounts of energy.

EDF Group operates the largest energy R&D facilities in Europe. Around 200 of the 2,000 or so researchers test applications of the latest equipment and technologies for cooling, heating, air-treatment, dryers and more. It's this knowledge we have available to transfer to our clients' own engineers to deliver leading edge energy saving techniques for their operations.

A commercial approach is employed. Our Advanced Efficiency Programmes are delivered as a bespoke business case and supporting action plan. It is built following in-depth energy audits of the company's energy intensive sites and processes by our specialist engineers. Recommendations are based on our own lab tests of equipment and techniques, rather than manufacturer claims. The detail goes much further than superficial surveys and reports, as does our support to ensure the projected savings are realised rather than be doomed to a filing cabinet.

Many clients were already efficient users as they operated energy intensive processes that demand attention for cost efficiency reasons as well as environmental considerations. Through our expertise, they have realised significant additional efficiencies and cost savings.

Energy efficiency for all businesses, great and small

At its most basic, energy efficiency is about making behavioural changes at an individual level. Everyone has a role to play in cutting waste in their immediate environment and these small changes can add up to a significant difference. But getting people to change their behaviour is tough – old habits die hard. Successful energy efficiency initiatives are well planned, not haphazard. Here are three key steps we recommend following:

1. Measurement

The basis of all energy efficiency campaigns is knowing how much, where and when you use energy in your business. Detailed measurement combined with a little detective work can provide valuable insights into where savings can be made. In fact, many managers are surprised when they first see how energy is used in their business, for example how much energy is used in unoccupied buildings overnight.

Measurement is essential for reporting results throughout your initiative. The more detailed your data, the better you can target your actions and report their successes. Data is available from bills, meters and dedicated energy monitoring services. Advice on how best to source and use data is contained in our Energy Efficiency Toolkit.

2. Creating a buzz

Effective campaigns have a clear communications programme that engages employees. This includes:

- a context for the initiative: why we're trying to save energy
- a clear explanation of what the company is trying to achieve: monetary, social and environmental objectives of the campaign in terms people can understand and hopefully visualise

- how staff can contribute: those desired behaviours such as switching off dormant equipment and being vigilant for waste

- regular reminders of how to contribute – those old habits die hard!

- feedback of how the initiative is progressing towards meeting its targets, and recognise the contribution of particularly dedicated staff.

Most of all, find someone in your business with a lot of personal energy and make them responsible for implementing the initiative and keeping the momentum going. Put the right tools in the hands of the right person and it's amazing what can be achieved. A wealth of communications materials are contained in our Energy Efficiency Toolkit. Best of all, these are customisable with your company logo and campaign message to help create a real sense of ownership and enthusiasm amongst your staff.

3. Show leadership and reward them

As a figure of authority in your business, you need to demonstrate you're as committed to energy efficiency as you expect your staff to be. Doing simple things like ensuring your own computer is switched off overnight and being visibly vigilant for waste encourages those around to do the same. And keep it up – changing behaviour takes time.

Rewarding your staff by sharing some of the savings your business achieves will reinforce positive behaviour. For example, some of the financial savings could boost the Christmas party fund, some could be donated to a local charity and some reinvested in energy efficiency.

Order your free copy of EDF Energy's efficiency toolkit by visiting: edfenergy.com/business.

You can find out about how our Advanced Efficiency Programmes have helped other businesses while you're there. See the targets we've set our own business by visiting edfenergy.com/ourvision.

DON'T GET LEFT

Today's consumers care about the future of our planet – and they demand the same from business. They need to know you are taking real action on climate change now and we can help you prove it.

A credible policy for addressing climate change better prepares your business for the future and raises your reputation as an industry leader. LRQA provides independent assurance of 'green' claims, helping to ensure that consumers recognise and trust your actions. Over the past 20 years we have been involved in creating global standards and processes that enable businesses to make a real, measurable difference in protecting the planet. We focus on using our worldwide expertise in verification, certification and assurance services to help our clients develop stewardship programmes that are relevant and credible.

Lloyd's Register Quality Assurance is a member of the Lloyd's Register Group

LRQA
Measure the Difference

BEHIND

12 Consumer trust

"Remember climate change in your brand planning. Consumers are highly sensitive to the stance that you take", say Anne Goodenough and Anne-Marie Warris at the Lloyd's Register.

Senior managers face a fundamental challenge: the uncertainty of predicting climate change and its associated risks to business; both direct, and as a result of how consumers and others respond to the challenges that climate change presents. Yet despite this uncertainty, decisions have to be made about how best to manage climate-related risks in order to avoid the biggest risk of all: 'ostrich' syndrome. Burying the corporate head in the sand and simply hoping that risks will disappear is no longer an option. Instead, it is imperative that climate change is viewed as a serious and imminent risk to business, with specific risk areas being identified and acted upon.

Around 80% of the FTSE100 companies now identify the effects of climate change as business risks. With this growing recognition has come an increase in corporate response, such that 65% of FT500 companies now have a board member who is responsible for climate change policy (Carbon Disclosure Project, 2007). But what should policies cover and how should plans be implemented so that they go beyond being a statement of intent and result in measurable strategies and appropriate action? An important, but often overlooked, component of managing climate change risk is building consumer trust in corporate sustainability. This chapter aims to increase corporate understanding of this technique by:

1. outlining the importance of building consumer trust in the sustainability of products and services;

2. discussing the wide-ranging advantages of embracing this as a climate risk management strategy;
and

3. exploring practical ways in which businesses can build consumer trust in their organisation.

The importance of building consumer trust

Increasingly, consumers are voting with their pockets and exercising 'green consumerism'. According to recent research, 96% of consumers now use environmental considerations in making purchase decisions, and two-thirds of customers are more likely to buy from businesses which address climate change risks. Contrary to widespread belief, many consumers are willing to pay a price premium for sustainable goods; for example, 33% of British consumers pay more for sustainably-harvested timber and 56% of Americans pay extra for ecologically-grown fruit. If climate change is becoming the mainstream consumer issue that the above statistics indicate, businesses need to examine ways in which they can build consumer trust in their sustainable policies. Given increased consumer awareness of climate change, companies which are able to build consumer trust in this regard are likely to enjoy an enhanced reputation, increased market share, and engender customer loyalty: factors which can combine to give considerable competitive advantage.

The role of businesses: proactive leadership or reactive compliance?

Despite the importance of building consumer trust, the role of business in managing the risks associated with climate change is still a subject of keen debate. Some maintain that it is up to governments to lead change by devising clear and transparent guidelines on how businesses should manage climate-related risks and that these should be enforced via regulation and fiscal measures to which businesses become reactively compliant. On the other hand, businesses have the opportunity to respond to the challenges of climate change in a proactive manner and help lead progress by working together with other interested parties, including governments, non-governmental organisations, and consumers. There is undoubtedly scope for a fundamental paradigm shift, such that companies no longer see climate change issues as threats to business but rather as challenges, or, even better, as opportunities. Progress is being made in this regard: encouragingly over 80% of FT500 companies now consider climate change to present commercial opportunities, including those afforded by increasing consumer trust in products and services.

Building consumer trust: the final step or the initial motivation?

Building consumer trust should not only be an exercise in public relations, it should be a catalyst for improvement within an organisation which can also have significant economic advantages. For example, in a case study of the snack food manufacturer Walkers, the Carbon Trust (2006) found that altering one aspect of manufacturing saved 9,200 tonnes of CO_2 and £1.2 million per annum. Thus, the process of building consumer trust can be both a means to an end and an end in itself.

Methods of building consumer trust

Building consumer trust as a strategy to reduce climate change risk is not very different from developing environmental polices and management systems, but with an increased emphasis on branding and publicity. It involves a company increasing its sustainability, validating claims made, and demonstrating this to consumers via eco-branding, publicity and sustainability performance reporting. This is not a linear progression, but rather a cyclical process of continual improvement.

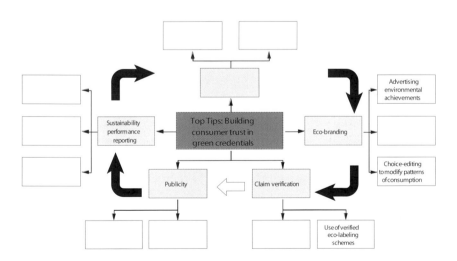

Top Tips: The process of building consumer trust in green credentials

Certification and verification

Use of globally-accepted management systems standards, such as ISO14001 and the greenhouse gas qualification, monitoring and reporting standards in ISO14064 are becoming increasingly recognised as a key method of managing corporate risks, including those of climate change. Such standards are important in building consumer trust in corporate sustainability in two ways: firstly, they facilitate identification of climate risks that can be mitigated in order to improve sustainability itself and secondly they demonstrate that such risks are being recognised and managed, thus enhancing consumer trust in corporate green credentials.

Eco-branding

Marketing of products and services according to their sustainability is becoming increasingly popular as a method of building consumer trust. As an example, Renault has recently launched a new line of environmentally-friendly vehicles. These are being marketed primarily on the basis of their green credentials, with a global advertising campaign that highlights the fact that all of the manufacturing has taken place in factories that are certified to the ISO14001 standard.

Choice-editing, whereby companies and/or governments phase out products that are unsustainable, also has potential. Although choice-editing is not necessarily advantageous in terms of achieving positive publicity – indeed consumers are sometimes frustrated by what they see as enforced changes to their purchasing – it can help organisations avoid damaging negative publicity for marketing unsustainable products when there is a better alternative. As an example, a major British supermarket recently launched a trial to phase out energy-inefficient light bulbs and electrical goods that do not carry a class 'A' rating.

Claim verification

Independent verification of claims is essential if consumers are to have faith in the validity of corporate sustainability statements. Indeed, 70% of people questioned in the recent 'What Assures Consumers on Climate Change?' report (AccountAbility, 2007) considered that third-party verification of climate change claims is of paramount importance. Claims can be verified by demonstrating compliance with approved standards. For example, specific claims about reduction in greenhouse gas emissions can be validated under ISO14064:1 or 2, while claims regarding energy efficiency can be validated by the Energy Efficiency Accreditation Scheme. Verified and independent eco-labelling schemes are another way in which green claims can be validated. Examples include the European eco-label ('the flower') and the more recent carbon emission label developed by the Carbon Trust. Any claims about sustainability must be able to withstand detailed review by consumer groups.

Publicity

While seeking good publicity is useful, avoiding negative publicity is imperative. Where corporate sustainability image is concerned, the concept that 'no publicity is bad publicity' could not be further from the truth. Unsustainable activities are newsworthy, particularly for major brands. In a recent poll, a British airline was voted the worst company for perceived environmental responsibility, a result which was probably influenced by negative publicity about the company's environmental impact immediately prior to the poll. Even more damaging is negative publicity as a result of non-compliance with legislation. This can result in loss of consumer trust which is more costly economically than the original fine.

Sustainability performance reporting

Performance reporting is another way in which corporations can disseminate information about the ways in which they are managing climate change issues, including carbon offsetting. It also provides a strategy for companies to identify areas for future improvement. Performance reporting initiatives include the Carbon Disclosure Project aimed at FT500 companies which now collects carbon information from 77% of the world's top 500 companies, and the Netherlands-based Global Reporting Initiative which has devised a suite of sustainability criteria, including energy use and greenhouse gas emissions, which are used by over 1000 organisations from around 60 countries.

Supply chain issues and challenges

Businesses face climate change risks not only as a result of their own actions and policies, but also through the activities of companies across their supply chains. In today's society, consumer trust in products is not won by companies simply addressing climate risk in their own operations. Instead, companies are held responsible, both by public opinion and the media, for sustainability throughout their supply chain. This life-cycle approach undoubtedly presents a major challenge to quantifying and managing climate-related risk, but is an issue which should not be ignored. The recent willingness of a major US software manufacturer to axe a supplier because it did not meet company standards, albeit in human rights rather than sustainability, demonstrates the importance of supply-chain thinking as part of corporate risk management. The move, which won the company a considerable amount of the positive media coverage essential in building consumer trust, is now being echoed by several leading UK supermarket chains in their attempts to manage climate change risk and build consumer trust in the effectiveness of this management.

Conclusions

Management of climate change risk has gone beyond being a useful 'add on' to company policy to become a fundamental consideration at all levels of a corporation, from the boardroom to the shop floor and every stage in-between, including in the supply chain. It is a subject that needs to be fully integrated into all business activities, including those such as branding, advertising and performance reporting which act as interfaces between corporate bodies and the consumer. The question is no longer can businesses afford to address climate change risk through initiatives to build consumer trust in their green credentials, but can they afford not to?

Key references

- AccountAbility (2007), *What Assures Consumers on Climate Change?* ISBN No: 1 901693 51 1

- Carbon Disclosure Project (2007), *Carbon Disclosure Project Report 2007: Global FT500.* Available online at: http://www.cdproject.net

- Carbon Trust (2006), *Carbon footprints in the supply chain: the next step for business.* London: The Carbon Trust.

The Lloyd's Register Group is an organisation that works to enhance safety and to approve assets and systems at sea, on land and in the air. We check that assets and systems work so that people and communities around the world can get on with everyday life. We are driven by a strong sense that what we are doing matters. To make this happen, we set, uphold and apply high technical standards of design, manufacture, construction, maintenance, operation and performance across many sectors to the benefit of many businesses.

Anne Goodenough is an environmental consultant for LRQA and a lecturer at the University of Gloucestershire where she teaches on the Environmental Management degree and postgraduate programmes. Contact: aegoodenough@glos.ac.uk

Dr Anne-Marie Warris is Technical Director - Climate Change for LRQA. She ensures the technical integrity of LRQA climate change services and liaises with external bodies and governments on climate change. She is the Vice-Chair of the UK Emissions Trading Group and authored the Voluntary Carbon Standard on behalf of the VCS Steering Committee. Contact: anne-marie.warris@lrqa.com

LRQA, member of the Lloyd's Register Group, is a leading independent provider of Business Assurance services. Our climate change services include validation and verification of carbon inventories, footprint and project emissions, as well as CSR report assurance. Voluntary and regulated carbon market schemes we cover include ISO14064, Voluntary Carbon Standard (VCS 2007), regional schemes, and Kyoto Protocol mechanisms, Clean Development Mechanism (CDM), Joint Implementation (JI) and the EU Emissions Trading Scheme.

We have over 25 years of experience in assessment and certification of quality, environmental and health & safety management systems. Our clients include large global organisations, bringing transparency and recognised assurance to their business processes and systems.

Lloyd's Register is an independent risk management organisation that works to help improve its clients' quality, safety, environmental and business performance throughout the world, because life matters.

13 Accounting for climate change

"For a business to move beyond the rhetoric and make sustainability climate change an integral part of its decision-making, they should be considering climate change in a strategic context", say Camilla Berens and Helenne Doody at CIMA.

It would be hard to think of two less likely bedfellows than accountants and eco-warriors. Environmentalists at the extreme end of the green spectrum may still view the finance function as the heartland of unsustainable corporate practices but more progressive thinkers are beginning to acknowledge that a radical deployment of the spreadsheet could be a far more effective tool in the drive towards sustainability than protests and placards.

From recent reports in the business pages, you could be forgiven for thinking that UK plc is now firmly committed to reducing its environmental impact. But despite the talk of offsetting, carbon footprints and triple bottom line reporting, it appears that we may be experiencing something of a false dawn. Behind the headlines and the glossy corporate brochures, only an enlightened few have taken up the green gauntlet. A survey of 209 senior executives from the FTSE350 and equivalent private companies carried out by KPMG last December (2007), found that 83% did not have a strategy in place for responding to global warming. In the international arena, a similar survey of more than 600 executives worldwide by the government-backed organisation, UK Trade and Investment, found that just one in ten businesses fully monitor their overall carbon impact.

The reasons for corporate inertia

One of the reasons for the current inertia may be that companies are waiting for the government to set the pace through regulation, taxation or cap and trade initiatives such as the forthcoming Carbon Reduction Commitment. But democratic governments are reluctant to take action which could be unpopular with the electorate, limit economic growth or damage their own country's corporate competitiveness in global markets.

Meanwhile, many businesses are still not considering the risks and opportunities associated with global warming. Too often climate change is pigeon-holed as a 'corporate responsibility' or 'investor relations' issue. Despite the high level of social awareness, the ramifications of climate change frequently fail to appear on a company's strategic radar. The current mindset is something along the lines of: "We're reducing our energy consumption and we're recycling. What more can we do?"

Sustainability from a different perspective

Climate change can be categorised under the broader heading of sustainability. CIMA's own sponsored research of 100 UK companies (Adams & Frost 2006) found a low level of quantified reporting, suggesting that sustainability is not taken into account systematically in decision-making. The flaw in the current mindset is the fact that CSR reporting fails to overcome the price mechanism's inability to communicate the real costs of externalities, in other words, a company's environmental impact. For companies to have a clear understanding of how they can move towards sustainability, the onus is on boards to carry out a full-scale strategic review. They should determine how the company's operations and products directly impact on the wider environment, not only in terms of income and costs but in relation to risk and opportunities, products and processes, brand positioning and intangibles, supply chains and business models.

A culture change is needed for sustainability to be accepted as good business practice, rather than a need to appease external stakeholders. It's about taking a long-term view of costs and income, risks and opportunities to ensure the company's enduring success. Once this mindset is in place, businesses will be able to move away from creative positioning and towards more effective methods of competitive positioning.

Enlightened management

There is a strategic imperative to address this issue sooner rather than later. It may be some time before regulation, taxation or cap and trade initiatives move towards internalising the externalities as real costs to a business. But these externalities already present risks to future demand. The real challenge is to address the strategic risks and opportunities ahead.

CIMA's forum of senior finance professionals contends that management accountants are in an ideal position to present this case to the board. Their training in financial analysis and risk management gives them the skills to provide directors with the management information needed to develop a robust and sustainable strategy. It's a question of management accountants recognising their potential and boards having the vision to realise it.

Evidently this is a huge challenge. There is no all-embracing solution and, however skilled, finance professionals cannot produce a panacea. But there are some tools that may help. The Enterprise Governance framework, developed by CIMA, in conjunction with the International Federation of Accountants (IFAC), can provide a useful mechanism for thinking about climate change in a strategic context. As illustrated in Figure 1, Enterprise governance helps organisations to focus on both conformance and performance aspects.

Generally, the conformance element takes a historic view and covers 'corporate governance'. Good corporate governance is not enough to make a company successful though. The performance dimension introduces forward looking aspects and highlights the importance of strategy and value creation.

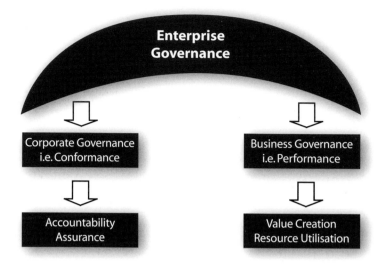

Figure 1: The Enterprise Governance Framework

In terms of sustainability and climate change, many organisations are looking only at the conformance components of the framework, reporting on and gaining assurance over historic activities in order to comply with regulations, risk management and customer expectations. The upside of risk should also be considered and this can be achieved through the performance dimension.

The performance aspect includes opportunities to save costs and develop new products, services and technologies to cater for changing needs, better meet customers' requirements and increase competitive advantage. Companies' time horizons need to be extended to consider the longer term impact of climate change, which lurks far beyond annual budget or three to five year strategic planning horizons.

Organisations need to take a long term view of the risks and the opportunities presented by climate change and adapt their strategy accordingly, balancing long-term value with short-term costs. Business can also be proactive in working with government to influence policy, so that it is in line with the organisation's long-term strategy, rather than taking the conformance approach of waiting for regulation to be imposed upon them.

The CIMA Strategic Scorecard™ may also provide a useful instrument for approaching climate change within a strategic context and preventing it from falling into a strategic blind spot. The scorecard is a pragmatic and flexible tool that is designed to help boards to engage more effectively in the strategic process. It is based on the premise that the management team is responsible for the detailed strategic planning, while the board needs to provide effective strategic oversight.

Too often management falls into the trap of focusing on more immediate matters rather than major long-term strategic issues. The scorecard gives the board a simple but effective tool for focusing attention on the most important strategic issues and for providing a constructive challenge to management by asking the right, searching questions.

To address the risk of a strategic blind spot, boards should maintain an issues log of the matters to be kept under review, while focusing on current issues and performance. As demonstrated in Figure 2, matters should be considered under the four headings in the model: Strategic Position; Strategic Risks; Strategic Opportunities; and Strategic Implementation.

Figure 2: The CIMA Strategic Scorecard™

A company's move towards sustainable development will only have real strength if management accountants are brought in at the beginning of the process. Their insight could provide vital support in helping to set the framework for discussion, assess the alternatives and define the business imperatives. Accountants may not look like the eco-warriors we see on our TV screens but given the opportunity, they may well be pivotal in implementing a quiet but radical revolution, not just in the finance function but across business as a whole.

Taking action

CIMA has put together a list of actions that can be taken by organisations, split into the dimensions of conformance and performance. These actions are aimed at boards, the wider management team and management accountants working together to incorporate climate change into strategy and day-to-day business life.

Conformance

1. Ensure compliance

As a minimum, organisations should ensure that they comply with any relevant legislation and regulations. For example, some activities require permits, licenses and exemptions. NetRegs provides free guidance on UK environmental regulations by business type and environmental topic (www.netregs.gov.uk). Organisations may also have to comply with requirements imposed by carbon trading schemes. Management accountants are likely to be in a position to provide the management information necessary to track the metrics required for monitoring and reporting on compliance.

2. Calculate your carbon footprint

Quantify your organisation's carbon footprint and track progress towards its reduction. Useful sources of guidance for calculating this include the Greenhouse Gas Protocol (www.ghgprotocol.org/) produced by the World Resources Institute (WRI) and the World Business Council for Sustainable

Development (WBCSD), ISO 14064 developed by the International Organization for Standardization's (www.iso.org/iso/home.htm) and the Carbon Trust (www.carbontrust.co.uk/solutions/carbonfootprinting/).

3. Conduct a risk assessment

Conduct a risk assessment in relation to climate change issues affecting your business. Areas to consider include the supply chain, potential regulation, reputational risk and customers' changing values. The risk assessment can be used to determine the organisation's objectives in relation to climate change, quantifying targets and influencing the organisation's strategy. The assessment should also help to identify actions to be taken over time to 'future-proof' the business against climate change risks, such as those presented by extreme weather conditions, escalating energy and resource costs, and eventually a low carbon economy.

4. Stakeholder analysis and reporting

Prepare a stakeholder analysis for determining the implications of climate change on the positioning of your brand. Consider the increased awareness of consumers and the growing focus of institutional investors on environmental issues. Report to stakeholders ensuring objectives, strategy and performance are made clear. Information may be tailored to meet the needs of environmentally aware investors and it may be useful to refer to the FTSE4Good Index (www.ftse.com/Indices/) or the Dow Jones Sustainability Index for more information (www.sustainability-indexes.com).

Performance

5. Identify opportunities and prepare a business case

Prepare a business case for developing the organisation's strategy to include opportunities arising from climate change. When assessing opportunities presented by climate change ensure competitive position, potential new products (or product improvement), new supply chain sources and new processes are considered. A proposition for changing the business model should be supported by a cost impact analysis and profitability forecasts. These should give focus to areas in which the organisation can successfully adapt its strategy, as well as influence the introduction of environmental policies such as the re-use of fleet cars, reducing business travel or energy-saving initiatives.

6. Long-term cost savings and efficiency improvements

Look for opportunities to continuously improve efficiencies and manage costs, especially in relation to energy, resource use, waste generation and recycling. A free publication is available from the Environment Agency to help accountants and financial managers identify key areas for cost-effective environmental improvement and increased profitability (http://www.envirowise.gov.uk/page.aspx?o=117664).

7. Internal charges for energy costs

Consider establishing a transfer pricing system for energy costs, so that the cost of energy is passed to the division using the energy. Raising internal invoices for energy costs creates an incentive for the users of energy to take actions to reduce energy usage, bringing down the overall costs and emissions for the organisation.

8. Value chain and life-cycle costing

Consider the entire value chain and life-cycle costing when investing in new processes and technologies and exploring new product opportunities. Such investments are likely to require capital investment appraisal, and climate change issues should be incorporated in the appraisal and the long term decision making process.

9. Introduce Sustainability KPIs

Introduce financial and non-financial KPIs to drive performance in these areas. This may include determining targets and metrics for tracking changes in brand value, monitoring cost saving and revenue opportunities from sustainability initiatives or measuring reduction in your organisation's carbon footprint. Defra (the Department for the Environment, Farming and Rural Affairs) has developed Key Performance Indicators (KPIs) for a wide range of sectors (http://www.defra.gov.uk/environment/business/envrp/). These KPIs provide a useful guide to the metrics that businesses could track.

10. Drive performance through environmental management information

Identify the management information needed to influence long term decision making with regard to climate change. The international standard on environmental management (ISO 14001) provides a framework for establishing an effective Environmental Management System (EMS) for integrating environmental responsibilities into day-to-day operations (www.bsigroup.com). By integrating environmental performance measures into financial processes to track savings and manage performance, measurement and reporting of environmental impacts will be tied into the decision making process.

Camilla Berens is the former news editor and chief feature writer of CIMA's monthly membership magazine *Financial Management*. She is now a freelance journalist specialising in green business development.

Helenne Doody is a specialist within CIMA's Innovation and Development department. She trained as an accountant with PricewaterhouseCoopers and has also worked in industry, focusing on risk management and internal control. Her areas of specialism include sustainability and climate change.

CIMA, the Chartered Institute of Management Accountants, is a world leading professional institute that offers an internationally recognised qualification in management accounting, with a full focus on business, in both the private and public sectors. It represents over 164,000 members and students in 161 countries. For further information please visit: www.cimaglobal.com

14 Environmental management systems

Impact. Targets. Control. Martin Baxter of the Institute of Environmental Management and Assessment assesses how international standards can be used to develop a structured framework in responding to climate change.

Many companies recognise the benefits of formal management systems to control certain aspects of their operations and International Standards have been developed to help organisations to structure their management to address issues such as quality, health and safety, and environment. This chapter explores how organisations can use environmental management systems (EMS) to help to meet the challenges of climate change.

For many companies, the challenges of climate change will be viewed as a series of controls that are placed on the amount of greenhouse gases (GHGs) that they emit from their operations either directly, or indirectly through their supply chain. Environmental management systems, such as the one set out in the international standard ISO 14001, are well developed tools for helping to identify and control emissions. However, viewing the challenge of climate change as purely an exercise in minimising the emissions of greenhouse gases misses two other important areas – the business opportunities that can be gained from effective management of environmental issues (and climate change impacts), and the business threat that might arise from a business strategy that isn't aligned to take account of a changing environment and climate change. Environmental management systems can help to ensure that these areas aren't overlooked.

Environmental management systems

An environmental management system is a structured framework for top management to improve the environmental performance of their organisation. The most widely recognised framework is that developed by the

International Organisation for Standardisation (ISO) in its standard *ISO 14001 – environmental management systems – requirements with guidance for use*. First published in 1996 and revised in 2004, over 140,000 organisations around the world have used ISO 14001 as the way to manage their environmental impacts. Key elements of an EMS, including ways of helping to ensure that climate change and greenhouse gas emissions are effectively managed, are described below.

Environmental policy

Central to an EMS is the environmental policy. The environmental policy is a declaration of the organisation's overall aims and principles with respect to the environment, as defined by its senior management. It must include a commitment to the continual improvement of environmental performance and to compliance with environmental legal and other requirements. The policy must also be publicly available.

An organisation's environmental policy should clearly acknowledge its impact on climate change (through emissions of GHGs) and the potential for climate change to impact on the organisation. Recognition of climate change at this policy level will help to ensure that appropriate management structures are implemented.

Identification and evaluation of environmental impacts

A key element of an EMS is the process of identifying and evaluating the organisation's impacts on the environment, and its activities, products and services that cause them (these are referred to as environmental aspects in ISO 14001). The evaluation is important as it ensures that the EMS is focussed on the environmental issues that really matter (those that are most significant) and that resources and management time are concentrated on controlling and improving them.

The identification of significant environmental aspects also needs to take account of the legislative, regulatory and other environmental requirements that affect the organisation. These may be pollution control permits, laws and regulations relating to the emissions of GHGs, or contractual requirements which specify environmental criteria required by customers of the organisation. For each of these significant environmental aspects, it is important that the EMS is set up to provide assurance to management and others who might have an interest (e.g. environmental regulators and customers), that they are being properly managed and that the organisation is able to comply with the requirements.

In terms of climate change, the organisation needs to identify those aspects of its activities, products and services that directly or indirectly result in emissions of GHGs. At this point, the organisation needs to take a broad view and consider upstream and downstream impacts – for example a TV manufacturer should identify that there will be GHGs emitted from manufacturing, from those making component parts in the supply chain, and that there will also be GHGs emitted as a result of the energy used by consumers watching TV. It's at this stage that some thought should be given to the extent to which climate change might affect your business – either in the long-term or short-term.

Short-term issues to consider might be in relation to flooding (think in terms of your own premises, those of you suppliers, or transport links between them), or drought conditions leading to water shortages. Longer term, you might need to look at climate scenarios and evaluate the extent to which your overall business model might be affected – if the UK is to develop a more Mediterranean style climate, this might have implications if you grow crops as existing varieties might not generate sufficient yields, or demand for your products that are influenced by certain weather patterns might decline.

Another important consideration will be the extent to which some climate change impacts are controlled by legislation. In some cases, restrictions are being placed on the amount of GHG emissions companies are legally entitled to emit. At present, these limits are largely being controlled through a financial trading mechanism. In other cases, legislation is being targeted to indirectly limit GHG emissions, for example legislation to make energy using products more efficient sets obligations on manufacturers. Given the high levels of political interest in climate change, it is likely that legislation around this subject will grow and companies will need to ensure that they know what applies to them and how this area of the law might develop in the future.

Assessment of significance

Assessing the significance of an environmental impact is one of the most challenging parts of environmental management. In many circumstances, professional judgement will play an important role in determining how to assess significance and this can be helped through consultation with appropriate stakeholders. The significance of an environmental impact, including those relating to climate change, can be assessed through consideration of:

- The size, nature, frequency, likelihood and duration of the environmental impact;

- the sensitivity of the receiving environment and the extent to which the impact is reversible;

- the extent to which the impact (or the activity, product or service which causes it) is covered by environmental laws and regulations, or contractual requirements; and

- the importance of the impact to interested parties – e.g. employees, neighbours, regulators.

Operational control, targets and objectives

The results of the identification and evaluation of the significance of the environmental impacts are used to identify operational control measures and to set objectives and targets for environmental improvement. Objectives and targets need to relate to the organisation's environmental policy and its environmental aspects. All significant environmental aspects will require operational controls to ensure that actions are carried out as planned and some of them will require objectives and targets for improvement.

Objectives are broad-based environmental goals that the organisation sets itself for environmental management and improvement. They may relate to a specific environmental issue, for example in climate change terms:

- to reduce the overall emissions of carbon dioxide equivalents (CO_2e) directly released by the organisation by 20% from the beginning of 2008 to the end of 2012.

Targets are detailed performance requirements that need to be met in order to achieve an overall objective. Where possible, objectives and targets should be SMART – Specific, Measurable, Achievable, Relevant and Time-related. This will help to track progress and ensure that achievements are being realised.

Environmental programme

An environmental programme turns the environmental objectives and targets into practical actions that can be taken to improve the organisation's environmental performance. The programme should identify individual responsibilities and the means to achieve the defined objectives and targets within the specified time scales. It should translate the commitment to continued environmental improvement set out in the environmental policy into practical actions.

Structure and responsibilities

The organisation's management will need to assign tasks to people so that everyone knows what has to be done. It is vital, if the EMS is to operate effectively, to know who does what, how, when and with what authority.

Whatever the size of the organisation, the activities of all employees will have an impact on the environment. Directly or indirectly, significant or small, everyone can contribute positively by innovating with new ideas, changing behaviour and involving other people. This will require information, training and the development of new skills.

Communication

An EMS relies on good communications for it to be effective. Internal communication needs to ensure that people are kept up to date with how progress is being made against environmental objectives and targets, and that they are able to influence the development of the EMS and environmental improvement programmes. External communications help to ensure that stakeholders are kept informed of the organisation's progress and can be engaged in the improvement process.

The increased attention on environment and climate change issues offers companies that are effective in reducing their impact an opportunity to enhance their competitiveness. New markets are emerging for those who operate responsibly, and consumers are becoming more interested in these issues. Once you've got the evidence to be able to demonstrate that you're taking the environment and climate change seriously, and that your performance is improving, this can become an important point as you position your organisation and products in the marketplace.

Procedures and documentation

The EMS must be documented and procedures need to be established to ensure that everyone knows how the system operates and what is required. Contrary to popular belief, ISO 14001 doesn't require extensive documentation. Long narrative procedures may be required in some circumstances, but a flow diagram might be equally effective in ensuring that a task is carried out properly. Wherever possible, organisations should build on existing systems and integrate environmental issues into them, rather than developing them separately.

Monitoring, audit and periodic evaluation of legal compliance

Information on the environmental performance of the organisation is essential if it is to track progress against its environmental objectives and targets. Without reliable and robust data, it can not be sure that it is in control of its environmental performance, or that performance is improving as intended. In many cases the organisation will already be carrying out measuring and monitoring activities, for example as a requirement of a pollution control licence, and should build on these in its EMS. In terms of climate change, it's important that appropriate measurement protocols and indicators are used. In some cases, conversions will need to be calculated to express energy consumption into a figure which represents an impact on climate change.

One of the important requirements in ISO 14001 is for organisations to carry out a periodic evaluation of legal compliance. This is a key task, which will help to inform the organisation on its performance against environmental laws and regulations, and provide information on whether it is adhering to its environmental policy. The frequency with which the organisation carries out the periodic evaluation should depend on the potential environmental impacts of the activity, with the most significant being checked more often than those of lesser importance.

Auditing helps to determine whether the planned elements of the EMS are being implemented as intended and that the EMS is functioning as planned. It also provides information to management on the overall performance of the system.

Management review

The EMS operates as a cyclical process of identifying, improving and checking. Periodic reviews by management ensure that the EMS is achieving the desired outcomes and that the environmental policy is being implemented. It will also provide a means for management to review the organisation's environmental performance trends to ensure that performance is being improved and to instigate changes to the system as necessary.

Conclusion

A structured management framework provides an effective means to address climate change impacts and EMSs are a ready made tool. As the financial cost of climate change becomes reflected in the prices that are paid for goods and services, those organisations that are able to become more 'eco-efficient' and reduce their environmental costs, will become more competitive. It will also help to enhance their reputation and become a more sustainable organisation.

Martin Baxter is the Institute of Environmental Management and Assessment's Deputy Chief Executive, with responsibility for strategy, governance and stakeholder liaison. Martin provides technical advice on environmental management systems to the Department for Environment, Food and Rural Affairs (Defra) and the European Commission, and forms part of the UK delegation to the International Organisation for Standardisation (ISO) in the area of environmental management. Martin also chairs the United Kingdom Accreditation Service (UKAS) Environmental Management Stakeholder Advisory Committee.

The Institute of Environmental Management and Assessment (IEMA) is the UK's largest membership and professional body supporting environmental practitioners. With a membership of over 13,000, the IEMA supports the development of practical skills and tools to help people improve environmental performance. Further information can be found at www.iema.net

Part 3

Managing physical risks

15 Adapting to climate change

"Heatwaves, floods, storms. The climate is already changing, so work out the potential damage it could cause to your business", says Kay Johnstone at the UK Climate Impacts Programme.

The vast majority of the business response to climate change has so far involved efforts to reduce greenhouse gas emissions and energy consumption. This type of activity is known as mitigation. There is another separate activity that will be required if businesses are to survive in the face of a changing climate, which is known as 'adaptation'. This chapter seeks to demonstrate that adaptation is an essential part of managing the climate risk by exploring the business case for adapting to unavoidable climate change. An overview of the process of adaptation is then provided, highlighting some available tools and resources.

The need to adapt as well as mitigate

Climate change cannot be avoided in the short-term. This is because of the long lifetime of CO_2 in the atmosphere, so that the warming we are experiencing now is a result of emissions from the last century. With a certain amount of climate change inevitable over the next few decades, adaptation is crucial, regardless of how successful we are at reducing greenhouse gas emissions.

Box 1: Definitions

> Mitigation: Tackling the causes of climate change by reducing greenhouse gas emissions.
>
> Examples of mitigation activities include energy efficiency, uptake of clean technologies or renewables, transport planning and provision of 'green' products or services.
>
> Adaptation: Responding to the projected impacts of climate change in order to reduce their adverse effects.
>
> Examples of adaptation measures include flood protection, improved summer cooling and business continuity planning.

The business case for adaptation

The drivers for mitigation and adaptation differ. Businesses undertake mitigation activities in order to improve resource efficiency, comply with regulations, voluntary codes or corporate social responsibility requirements or to improve green credentials. This in turn contributes to the overarching goal of protecting future generations from dangerous climate change. Adaptation, on the other hand, is about protecting your own business from the negative effects while making sure you are in a position to benefit from any positive impacts.

The past is full of examples of how the weather can disrupt economic activity. In 2006 more than 50% of UK business suffered disruption as a result of extreme weather. Storms at the end of November caused widespread disruption, while heatwave conditions in the summer forced some to shut down computers or close offices (Woodman, 2007). The summer floods of 2007 also had dramatic effects on UK businesses. Many suffered stock and equipment losses and failures of power and communications leading to lost orders. Effects on trade were particularly serious for small businesses (Pitt, 2007).

Single weather events, such as these, cannot be attributed to climate change. However, it is known that climate change will drive an increasing frequency of such events (Hulme et al., 2002). SMEs are potentially more vulnerable to the climate risk than larger companies, having fewer resources to withstand the impacts (Howlin and Ezingeard, 2005).

Table 1 lists some of the ways in which climate change will result in direct costs, business continuity and productivity issues and wider changes to the operating environment. Customers and supply chains often represent a large proportion of the exposure of an SME to the climate risk due to their large geographical coverage relative to the company's own operations. Therefore, impacts on these aspects are likely to feature prominently. The trend for 'just in time' delivery systems increases vulnerability to supply chain impacts.

advisors, government or sector representatives (Howlin and Ezingeard, 2005; Berkhout et al., 2004; Lucey, 2006).

The UK Climate Impacts Programme is funded by the UK Government to assist organisations in understanding and preparing for the impacts of climate change. UKCIP advocates a dynamic risk based approach to adaptation and has developed an online Adaptation Wizard for assisting organisations through the adaptation process. The process is shown in figure 1 and is based on the more technical Risk, Uncertainty and Decision-Making Framework (Willows and Connell, 2003).

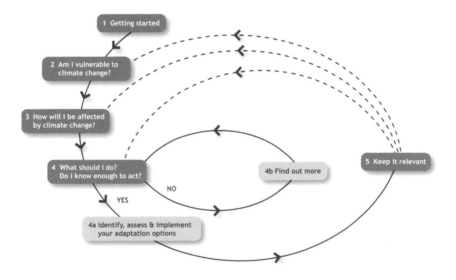

Figure 1: The UKCIP Adaptation Wizard five-step process.

Where to start

The purpose of adaptation depends on your priorities and which aspects of your business you are trying to protect or enhance. For example, depending on the nature of your market and whether you are trying to maximise profit or market share, you may have a different attitude to the loss of business continuity. It is, therefore, important to think carefully about what you are trying to achieve and set objectives. However, this is often a difficult task without a broad understanding of what climate risks are faced. A quick brainstorming exercise on what the future climate might mean, for example by using UKCIP's Business Areas Climate Assessment Tool (BACLIAT) (Metcalf and Jenkinson, 2003), is therefore a good starting point. As well as using future climate scenarios to imagine the types of impacts that might be faced, it is also useful to draw on past experience of extreme weather events either on yourself or others within your sector or supply chain.

Planning and implementing a response

Adaptation measures include those that involve delivering adaptation actions and those that build adaptive capacity. Adaptation actions include technical fixes, strategic solutions or changes in working practices that protect some aspect of the business (staff, process, finances etc), enable a quick recovery or exploit a new opportunity. Adaptive capacity, on the other hand, is the information, social capital and supportive conditions that are needed as a foundation for delivering adaptation actions. UKCIP's adaptation actions database contains details of existing adaptation activities of all types.

Potential adaptation measures should be evaluated against initial objectives, whilst taking into account the non-climate future. Since there is uncertainty attached to the impacts of climate change, the organisation's attitude to risk will play a part in deciding which options to pursue. Some options will provide benefits in excess of their costs whatever the extent of climate change. For example, where a business already suffers from the impacts of weather, then many adaptation measures will fall into this category and benefits will be felt immediately. There may also be options that represent 'win-wins' by contributing to other objectives as well as adaptation to climate change.

Climate change is not a one-off event but is a continuous process of change in the context of many socio-economic changes. Adaptation to climate change must also therefore be a dynamic process. Strategies or plans should be reviewed regularly to make sure they are still relevant and to allow for the incorporation of new information. Most adaptation measures can be integrated with other systems and procedures, such as the existing risk register, health and safety arrangements, quality management, business continuity planning or strategic planning. In this way the impacts of climate change can be managed like any other business risk in a manner that is proportionate, relevant and cost-effective.

The Adaptation Wizard and all other UKCIP tools are available at www.ukcip.org.uk.

References

Berkhout, F, Hertin, J and Arnell, N (2004) *Business and Climate Change: Measuring and Enhancing Adaptive Capacity*. Tyndall Centre Technical Report 11. Tyndall Centre Technical Reports are available online at: http://www.tyndall.ac.uk/publications/tech_reports/tech_reports.shtml

Chrichton, D (2006) *Climate change and its effects on small businesses in the UK*. Published by AXA Insurane UK plc. ISBN 978-0-9554108.

Hulme,M., Jenkins,G.J., Lu,X., Turnpenny,J.R., Mitchell,T.D., Jones,R.G., Lowe,J., Murphy,J.M., Hassell,D., Boorman,P., McDonald,R. and Hill,S. (2002) *Climate Change Scenarios for the United Kingdom: The UKCIP02 Scientific Report*, Tyndall Centre for Climate Change Research, School of Environmental Sciences, University of East Anglia, Norwich, UK. 120pp

Howlin, N, Ezingeard, J (2005) *Out of Business as Usual: The Challenge of Business Continuity Management in the UK's Small and Medium Enterprises*. Commissioned by AXA Insurance UK plc. Available at: http://www.axa4business.co.uk/bc/challenges.asp

Lucey, KA (2006) *Why Traditional Business Continuity Thinking Does Not Work for SMEs: A New Approach for Managers and their Advisors. Journal of Business Continuity and Emergency Planning*, 1 (1) 65-79.

Metcalf, G and Jenkinson, K (2005) *A Changing Climate for Business: Business Planning for the Impacts of Climate Change*. UKCIP, Oxford.

Pitt, M (2007) *The Pitt Review: Learning Lessons from the 2007 floods, Interim Report*. Crown Copyright. Ref: 284668/1207.

Stern, N (2006) *The Economics of Climate Change: The Stern Review*. Cabinet Office – HM Treasury. Cambridge University Press.

Willows, RI and Connell, RK (Eds) (2003) *Climate Adaptation: Risk, Uncertainty and Decision-making*. UKCIP Technnical Report. UKCIP, Oxford.

Woodman, P (2007) Business Continuity Management. Published by the Chartered Management Institute in association with the Cabinet Office and Continuity Forum. London.

The UK Climate Impacts Programme (UKCIP) helps organisations and decision-makers understand and prepare for the impacts of climate change. Based at the University of Oxford, UKCIP was set up by the Government in 1997 and is funded by the Department for Environment, Food and Rural Affairs (DEFRA). UKCIP offers a range of tools, resources and support to assist in assessing the impacts of climate change and adapting accordingly. Advice and support throughout the process is free of charge, on the understanding that any study findings and experience gained will be publicly available and fed back into UKCIP resources. For more information see www.ukcip.org.uk.

Kay Johnstone is responsible for delivering the programme for climate change impacts and adaptation with UK businesses. This involves working directly with private sector companies as well as with organisations that represent and support the business community, through partnerships, projects and capacity building activities. She has five years experience in the environmental sector with involvement in both practical environmental management projects and research activities. She can be contacted at kay.johnstone@ukcip.org.uk.

16 Natural hazards

Severe weather events are becoming more frequent.
Malcolm Goodwin and Simon Wong at ABS Consulting discuss
how to make the climate an integral part of the risk register.

Let's face it. For most CEOs, there are more pressing day-to-day issues
for you to be addressing than worrying about climate change. But an indefi-
nite postponement of the decision to put it on the agenda might, at best,
be negligent but fortuitously tolerable, and at worst lead to an undermining
of the current business whilst the competition seizes the opportunities
presented by climate change. Here we explore the issue of climate change
and an approach to consider to embrace its effects.

Yesterday's worry was the run on your share price due to malicious
unfounded rumours. What made it worse was this possibility was not even
recognised on your risk register, and your response had to be a little bit
more spontaneous than you would have preferred. Tomorrow's worry may
be similarly unpredicted, but it would be better if it is something that you
have already identified and to which you have given due consideration.
With a little preparation, the effects of climate change can be, and probably should be, appearing on your risk register, and allow you to relax.

To reach this state of relaxation and only then be justifiably complacent, it
is necessary to identify where climate change could have an influence on
your business and analyse the effects, possible problems and opportunities.

The meteorological effects

The quintessential Englishman talks about the weather for good reason
– it is very variable. We do not expect one summer in the UK to be the same
as the previous one. So a change in the average summer or winter temperature has no real direct relevance. In other parts of the world, the weather
might be a little more predictable with less variation, and a change to the
average temperatures is more directly discernable.

For some effects of climate change, it is the slow shift of the mean away from its historical values that is of relevance; some crops cannot effectively grow where they used to thrive. For other effects it is the severity or frequency of the extreme events that are changing; the 1 in 100 year event is drifting towards becoming the 1 in 25 year event, and the new 1 in 100 year event is much more severe than previously. Design parameters used by many codes that are based on the statistical analysis of historical data will always be inaccurate and suffer a time lag if the underlying trend of the data is not stable.

Meteorological effects, the severity and frequency of which are influenced by climate change, may cover:

Direct effect	Consequence
Hurricane/Typhoon/ Windstorm	Direct wind damage and missile damage. Storm surge and coastal flooding. Surface water flooding. Soil erosion/landslide/mudslide.
Tornado	Direct wind damage and missile damage.
Hailstorm	Impact damage.
Rainstorm/prolonged precipitation/deluge	Flash flood. Fluvial flood.
Extreme temperatures/ heatwave	Air, river water and sea water temperature extremes.
Drought	Reduced river flow rates; increased pollution concentration levels.

The impact of one or more of these effects on a business will depend on the type of business it is, where in the world it operates, and whether the business is already 'hardened' to cater for these consequences on a more frequent and more severe basis.

The impact can also be positive, creating opportunities for those positioned to recognise and prepare for them.

The traditional code based approach of meeting the minimum design requirements for the meteorological effects would raise several interesting questions with respect to the expected design life or usage for the facility, such as:

- The long-term justification for the chosen siting of the facility;
- Specification of the building envelope/infrastructure;
- Specification of equipment operating regimes/limits.

These engineering-related issues for the business can be addressed by setting up a clear understanding of the performance standards to be developed and complied with, with respect to climate change, as follows:

- Continued operation
- Immediate occupancy
- Life safety

The performance standards are particularly important for corporations with worldwide operations, the facilities of which are more likely to be exposed to varying levels of climate change effects according to their location.

CEO concerns

Whether driven by corporate governance requirements, preserving stakeholder value, you will have already addressed the company's stance, attitude, risk appetite and priorities in the following areas:

- Business interruption
- Life safety
- Brand reputation
- Risk reduction/risk transfer

In addressing the potential impact of the consequences arising from climate change for your business, the influences on these same aspects should be probed. Climate change may create entries in your risk register that will require a change in the company's risk appetite to be made, or for facilities and operations to be hardened in a general sense in order to mitigate the risk.

For new projects, or expansion of existing operations, the opportunity exists of specifying requirements at small additional cost that will suitably cater for climate change effects.

Some example considerations

Business model

Is your business model sensitive to climate change?

- Where do you operate?
    - In which countries and how will climate change affect these countries?
- What are your inputs and raw materials?
    - Will these continue to be available?
    - At what price?
    - Should alternative technologies be considered to still service your clients, because of the influence of climate change on the availability and price of raw materials?
- Will the demand change for your products and services?

For example, an industry heavily dependent on sugar beet production might be unfavourably influenced by climate change if the traditional producers of sugar beet found that climate change was influencing its viability.

A pharmaceutical company producing anti-malaria drugs might be presented with a changing population being affected by malaria, if the geographical spread of malaria changed with the changing climate.

Buildings

- Are your buildings located in areas where they would be more strongly influenced by more frequent and more severe meteorological-driven natural hazard events?
- Should the effect of natural hazards, and their possible worsening effects due to climate change, be one input into your long-term strategy of where in the world you choose to operate your key facilities?

- When performing major structural maintenance (eg cladding replacement to buildings), should this be performed to a higher requirement than local codes dictate in order to be compatible with the company's risk strategy, with a suitable margin to accommodate climate change effects?

Equipment and support services

- Are changing environmental conditions, such as ambient air temperature, river water volumes or temperatures, or sea water temperatures, going to affect your ability to operate, or your efficiency of operations?

A heavy industrial plant dependent on river water for cooling may have to reduce production in times of low river water flow or high river water temperature, in order that its effect on the river remains within prescribed limits.

A plant making controlled effluent discharges into a river may have to curtail operations if a reduced river flow leads to concentrations above tolerable limits.

A coastal power production plant may find itself with undersized cooling plant if sea temperatures rise beyond the values foreseen in the original design specification, leading to increasing regular reduction in output capability.

Changes to sea life due to sea water temperature changes can disable facilities reliant on sea water cooling due to clogging of screens and filters with 'invasions' of jellyfish or shoals of fish beyond that originally envisaged.

Refrigeration plant or HVAC plant on a more frequent basis may prove to be undersized to operate at capacity during times of heatwave.

Combating the effects

Once the exercise has been undertaken to review your business for the effects of climate change, then what are the options for addressing the issues raised?

Continue to monitor

This could be viewed as an euphemism for 'do nothing', but it is not. It is probable that many major business model decisions will be made within the timescales associated with climate change. The process of recognising a potential issue associated with climate change, and to be continuing to monitor it, will have a small but proportionate influence on these key business decisions to be taken in the future.

Seize the opportunity

Where climate change presents an opportunity, take the basis of the opportunity forward to give it the time and investment, as per any other business opportunity.

Process the changing risk

The recognition and processing of the changing risk might be through:

- accepting the increased risk;
- implementing a programme of upgrade to chosen performance requirements at key facilities, where the risk is incompatible with the company's appetite for risk;
- risk transfer.

Embody climate change consideration in upgrade and new build work

An informed decision to deliberately over-specify the withstand or performance requirements can future-proof the facility with respect to the influence of climate changes. For the maintenance/upgrade of existing facilities, the specification of a higher demand requirement is only worthwhile if the vulnerability is one of the controlling vulnerabilities for the peril being considered, or it forms part of a site-wide systematic approach.

Suggested overall approach for CEOs to instigate

To effectively incorporate the effects of climate change into a business's systems, both for its own benefit and to be demonstrating to stakeholders that it is appropriately addressing any corporate governance requirements, the key steps below are recommended:

1. Develop a review methodology with the affected parties.

2. Using the latest knowledge, assess if there is an increased probability of any event occurring.

3. Assess if there is the potential for a higher severity of event.

4. Assess if there is a significant change in risk due to climate change.

5. Process the risk through normal channels within the business, recording the acceptance, mitigation to appropriate performance levels, or risk transfer decision.

6. Update Business Continuity Plans where the mitigation requires it.

7. Consider any opportunities identified to the business identified by climate change.

Climate change historically may have been low on a CEO's agenda, but its consideration cannot afford to be put to one side indefinitely. By a company reviewing its effects and including entries in a business risk register, then the effects can be recognised and periodically reviewed. With this in place, the company's normal business processes can address the risks arising from climate change, as per any other risk or opportunity to its business.

ABS Consulting Ltd is the head office for ABS Consulting European Operations and is part of ABS Group of Companies, Inc. Its purpose is to expand and diversify the consultancy activities of ABS Group by offering risk management, safety assessment, environmental consulting, quality and certification services to a wide range of industries and companies headquartered or based in Europe. The Europe head office is located in Warrington, UK. Further details:

mgoodwin@absconsulting.com
swong@absconsulting.com
www.absconsulting.com/europe/

17 Flooding

"Flooding is a real and growing danger", says Sarah Youren at Field Fisher Waterhouse, "but where does responsibility lie for keeping developments dry?"

We saw horrendous flooding in summer 2007 which the Association of British Insurers estimate has cost the industry around £3 billion in claims and, according to the climate change experts, we can only expect these extreme weather conditions to get worse in the future. How then do you plan development to try and ensure that your new project stays dry? Who is responsible for building and maintaining flood defences? How much should developers be contributing to the cost of flood defence works? Should we be building in areas at risk of flooding at all?

Finding the right location – PPS 25

The Government published *Planning Policy Statement 25: Development and Flood Risk* in December 2006. The thrust of PPS 25 is to direct development which would be most vulnerable to flooding away from areas at highest risk of flooding. When local planning authorities make a decision on a planning application, the policies in PPS 25 will be a material consideration that they must take into account and they will override any policies in their local plan which have not already been updated to take account of PPS 25.

Flood zones

PPS 25 divides all land in the UK into three zones according to the likelihood of that land flooding from rivers or the sea. It ignores the presence of flood defences as these may be breached, overtopped or may not be in existence for the lifetime of the development. Zones 2 and 3 are shown on the Environment Agency flood map and zone 1 is everything that is left. Zone 1 comprises land assessed as being least likely to flood, zone 2 is more likely to flood and zone 3a is more likely still, with zone 3b being the functional floodplain.

PPS 25 then identifies different land use groups and assesses how vulnerable to flooding they would be. Water compatible uses would be things like marinas, open space, nature conservation areas and outdoor sports and recreation uses. Basement dwellings and mobile homes are considered to be highly vulnerable uses. More vulnerable uses would be uses such as hospitals, houses, hotels and educational facilities. Less vulnerable uses would be shops, offices, general industry, warehousing, restaurants and leisure uses.

In principle, land within a particular zone is only suitable for certain specified land uses as set out in a table in Annex D in PPS 25. For example, all uses of land are appropriate in zone 1. In zone 2 all uses other than highly vulnerable uses are permitted. In zone 3a water compatible uses and less vulnerable uses are acceptable. More vulnerable uses may be permitted in zone 3a only if the exception test is passed. Highly vulnerable uses should not be permitted in zone 3a. In zone 3b only water compatible uses and essential infrastructure that has to be there will be permitted. Essential infrastructure would have to pass the exception test.

The sequential test

A sequential risk based approach is taken to determine suitability of land for development in flood risk areas. In areas at risk of river or sea flooding local authorities should try to locate new development in flood zone 1. If there is no reasonably available site in flood zone 1 then flood zone 2 and then 3 can be considered, taking into account whether it would be an appropriate location for the type of use sought. Within each flood zone new development should be directed to sites at the lowest probability of flooding from all sources. Local planning authorities should only allow development in areas of flood risk where there are no reasonably available sites in areas of lower flood risk, and the benefits of the development outweigh the risk from flooding.

The exception test

If, following application of the sequential test, it is not possible to locate development in zones of lower probability of flooding, the exception test can be applied to manage flood risk while still allowing necessary development to take place. All three elements of the exception test will have to be passed in order for development to be permitted.

To pass the exception test:

a) it must be demonstrated that the development provides wider sustainability benefits to the community that outweigh the flood risk;

b) the development should be on developable brown field land if available;

c) a flood risk assessment must show that the development will be safe without increasing flood risk elsewhere and where possible will reduce flood risk overall.

Housing in the floodplain

This would seem to indicate that, for example, housing could not be located in zone 3b at all and only in zone 3a if there are no suitable sites in zones 1 and 2 and the exception test could be passed. However, the Government is sending out rather mixed messages as the Housing Green Paper says that building housing on floodplains should be avoided if better alternatives can be found in the same area but certainly does not rule it out altogether and Housing Minister Yvette Cooper said in July this year that given the number of new homes required some of them will have to be built on floodplains subject to appropriate flood defences being in place.

Businesses in the floodplain

Business uses such as offices, general industry and warehousing are classed as less vulnerable uses so these can be sited in zones 1, 2 or 3a. This gives a wide range of choice as to where to site your new development but gives no guarantee that it won't flood. You would therefore be well advised to consider firstly the best ways to prevent water entering the building which may include measures such as soakaways built into the landscaping of the site, siting the building on a slightly raised part of the site or flood shutters at ground level.

Secondly, you should consider the best ways to minimise the damage if water does enter the building. Can you use the ground floor and any basement areas for uses such as parking rather than expensively decorated meeting rooms? Can you locate electrical systems, radiators, boilers above the likely flood level? Historically many companies kept their server rooms in the basement, however this is the worst possible location in the event of a flood as the business impact of loosing vast amounts of data will be costly. Equally, businesses that store stock or expensive machinery at ground or basement level run the risk of massive losses in the event of a flood.

All businesses should find out whether their existing premises are at risk of flooding as well as any proposed new premises. If they are then they should prepare a flood plan. The Environment Agency website has a useful template for preparing a flood plan and advises that by planning ahead most businesses can save 20-90% on the cost of lost stock and moveable equipment, as well as saving themselves considerable time, effort and hassle. Don't forget that you will also be responsible for the safety of your staff so should include training on an evacuation plan in your flood planning process.

Responsibility and funding

Interestingly, local planning authorities, the Environment Agency and other operating authorities have powers to build and maintain flood defence structures but are not under a statutory duty to carry out or maintain flood defence works in the public interest. Flood defence schemes are funded at least in part by central Government but funding is limited so urgently needed projects can take years to get to the top of the funding list.

Landowners have the primary responsibility for safeguarding their land and property against flooding. They are also responsible for managing the drainage of their land in such a way as to prevent adverse impacts such as flooding from run off to adjacent land. This, taken with the emphasis in PPS 25 that flood risk measures must be sufficiently funded to ensure safe occupation of the site throughout its lifetime, means that Council's will increasingly be looking to developers to pay for what some would consider to be essential infrastructure.

The Government announced on 13 February 2008 that it is undertaking a fundamental review, with the insurance industry, into the principles on which they commit to continuing to offer existing customers flood insurance where the flood risk is adequately managed. The review is expected to be finalised in summer 2008. The Association of British Insurers has indicted that continued availability of flood insurance cover is dependant on "major new total investment from the Government and others".

With insurance companies making noises about withdrawing insurance for flooding in high risk areas, it is clear that flood prevention schemes must go ahead, but if the Government is looking to push too much of this cost onto developers they run the risk that new development schemes become financially unviable. For example, with the current push to create three million new homes by 2020, some of which the Government admits must be located in areas at risk of flooding, it is arguable that the Government must play its part in funding flood defences. In the pre-budget report the Government has pledged to increase flood defence spending from £600 million in 2006/7 to £800 million by 2010/11 but no commitment has been made for the intervening years which could mean a four year delay in additional funding.

Sarah is a Partner in the Planning and Environment team at Field Fisher Waterhouse. She advises on all aspects of planning and environmental law from inception to construction of a project. Her clients include private developers, funders, local authorities and Government organisations.

The Planning and Environment team advise on all aspects of planning and environmental law. We have a particular interest in sustainable development and help clients obtain planning permission, evaluate Environmental Impact Assessments, negotiate planning and infrastructure agreements and acquire sites through compulsory purchase. On the environmental side we offer skilled and commercial advice on issues such as flooding, contaminated land, waste, water pollution and recycling. We have considerable experience in the energy field and with flood related development.

Further details: www.ffw.com

Part 4

Emissions control

153

18 How carbon markets are working

Carbon markets are evolving quickly, creating a new financial
toolbox that will take climate change policies to the next stage,
Greg Dunne at ICECAP reports.

2008 is a landmark year for the development of international carbon markets,
a key tool for the management of climate risk, as it marks the beginning
of the compliance period for signatories to the Kyoto Protocol and the first
steps in a 'roadmap' towards a global climate change agreement by late
2009.

The years leading up to 2008 have tested and proven the use of market
mechanisms as a means to manage and limit global emissions. The legal
and policy surround has been created, the market infrastructure has been
designed and implemented, the market has been populated by the key actors
such as emitters, finance houses, exchanges and speculators, much of the
physical market has become liquid with the development of derivatives and
structured products following closely behind and, above all, a continuously
updated carbon price is available at least in Europe.

At the same time, policy and market developments have not always moved
in tandem and a lack of policy for a post-2012 accord has created market
volatility. Changes in the policy position of European legislators may potentially disrupt the market, for example, by proposing to close the European
market to new supply of emissions credits from the flexible mechanisms
of the Kyoto Protocol. Finally, the continued lack of participation in the
market from the USA, the largest emitter of greenhouse gases in the world
(by some accounts already being overtaken by China), makes little sense
in a scheme that was designed to include the US and introduces serious
imbalances on the demand side of the market.

The theoretical basis for emissions trading as a mechanism for reducing
greenhouse gas emissions with an end goal of controlling climate change

derives from environmental economics. The essential principal is that emissions trading should reduce the cost of compliance for those actors subject to reduction targets. For example, if the cost of abatement per tonne of carbon bears a cost of $5 to Emitter A and a cost of $10 to Emitter B, it follows that in a perfectly liquid market with no transaction costs the carbon price will be $7.50. In this way, Emitter A is incentivised to over-achieve its targets and can profitably sell its surplus to Emitter B and, in turn, Emitter B can reduce its cost of abatement by buying from Emitter A. Both emitters will continue to trade with each other until the cost of abatement and the cost of carbon reach parity. This is known as the 'lowest cost solution'.

This principal can be demonstrated with respect to the two principal emissions markets which exist today, namely the European Emissions Trading Scheme (EU ETS) and the Clean Development Mechanism (CDM), while providing an overview of their main characteristics.

The EU ETS started its life in 2003 as a result of the adoption and implementation in EU member states of the EU Emissions Trading Directive. The Directive is the principal measure for the member states of the European Union to achieve a reduction in emissions of 8% from a 1990 baseline by the end of the Kyoto Compliance period in 2012. The 8% figure represents the aggregate reduction across Europe and is applied to each member state with regard to its specific circumstances, some having lower or higher targets.

The scheme is divided into two phases – 2005 to 2007 and 2008 to 2012, the first phase being effectively a prototype. It imposes emissions reduction obligations on approximately 12,000 installations responsible for about 45% of Europe's CO_2 emissions. The installations are predominantly drawn from the power sector together with many of the emissions-intensive industrial sectors such as oil, steel and cement.

Each installation is allocated allowances equivalent to its target, which is designed to create appropriate scarcity in the market. The allowances are formulated prior to each phase by the EU member states under guidelines set out by the European Commission. Each member state is required to clearly demonstrate how its allocation of allowances, together with other national measures, allows it to reach its Kyoto target. Most allowances are free with a small amount of discretion for auctioning.

Each installation is newly required to apply for a (non-tradable) permit to emit greenhouse gases and thus take part in the EU ETS. The 'permit' is issued subject to installations having in place a comprehensive emissions monitoring and reporting capability. In addition, emissions are independently verified annually at installation level prior to being surrendered against targets. Each member state has a registry in which the installations hold accounts to which their allowances are credited and allowances can subsequently be transferred when purchased or sold. The registry allows the installations, EU member states and the EU itself to monitor compliance against targets at all levels of the EU ETS.

In view of the rapid development and deployment of policy described above and the sophisticated infrastructure put in place, has the EU ETS been a success? Clearly, the achievements of the scheme in the face of its ambitious scope and pace of implementation are many. Notably, there is now a fully functioning market in which liquidity is increasing by step changes annually. In 2007, 1.6bn tonnes changed hands with a financial value of €28bn (362m tonnes with a value of €7.2bn in 2005) according to Point Carbon. With respect to price behaviour, the first phase of the EU ETS saw dramatic price falls owing to over allocation of allowances and, more controversially, high electricity prices as power companies appeared to pass on carbon costs despite allowances being free. However, the EU Commission has stood firm on phase 2 and imposed stricter reduction targets now that reliable data is available on European emissions output and there are few acceptable arguments for lobbying in the light of the collapse of the phase 1 price. In summary, the EU ETS is implementing a scheme which looks set to achieve its policy aims while showing all the volatility of an early stage financial market.

One of the key policy measures for Europe to achieve its Kyoto targets in the most cost effective way was the implementation of the European Linking Directive in 2004. This enabled Europe to link to the Clean Development Mechanism (CDM) allowing access by its emitters to credits from developing world projects. Theoretically, it should always be cheaper to fund abatement activities in the developing world than in the developed world and the EU estimated that linkage should reduce the costs of Kyoto compliance to its emitters by about 25%. At the time of writing, CDM credits can be obtained from creditworthy counterparties in the European secondary market at a discount of 25-30 per cent depending on the vintage, so EU policy-makers can make a case for having achieved their aims.

The CDM has grown enormously since the EU Linking Directive was implemented, one of the key drivers for its growth being European demand. The CDM is overseen by the CDM Executive Board (EB) which is contained within the United Nations Framework Convention on Climate Change (UNFCCC) organisation in Bonn and reports annually to the UNFCCC Conference of the Parties (COP) held in different locations. The EB is supported by a secretariat which administers the complex and lengthy processes associated with the registration of projects and issuance of credits. The secretariat is now funded principally by fees levied on the participants in the projects having initially been funded by parties to the UNFCCC.

The CDM is a project based mechanism whereby emissions reduction projects which are proven to be 'additional' to business-as-usual practice in that country, are eligible for carbon finance. Carbon finance in this sense means the additional capital which can be deployed in the project as a result of the sale of the credits. In this way, projects which would not provide a viable or acceptable rate of return may achieve desired investment benchmarks through the additional finance from the carbon markets. This is the concept of 'additionality' which must be substantially elaborated for each project in addition to its baseline, i.e. the difference between emissions output under a business-as-usual project and the CDM project. The difference between the emissions from the baseline scenario and the actual emissions from the project are quantified emissions reductions which can be sold into the international markets.

The concepts just outlined are central to the complex regulatory framework for the CDM and each project undergoes a cycle in several steps which includes validation and documentation of the project, approvals by governments to release and receive the credits, monitoring of the emissions reductions, verification and certification of the credits by independently accredited entities, and concludes with the issuance of the credits by the CDM EB.

The growth in the market is partly attributable to the development of a range of methodologies which have been approved at CDM EB level, each methodology enabling multiple projects to be undertaken using that methodology. The methodologies now encompass most well-known abatement technologies globally, including renewable energy, fuel switching in the power industry, reductions in industrial process emissions, capture of waste gases for destruction, conversion or reuse and management of biodegradable waste.

The CDM market has become a popular source of foreign direct investment particularly for rapidly industrialising countries such as China and India. In addition, it has driven technology transfer by enabling unviable projects and building capacity for new technologies. It is an attractive hedging mechanism for companies and governments with liabilities under the Kyoto Protocol with an appetite for emerging market risk, and many find it complimentary to existing project financing, inward investment or international development programs.

As a result the market has grown exponentially with a pipeline of 2.3bn credits from validated projects at the end of 2007 (1.6bn at the end of 2006) according to UNEP. Formal market mechanisms are mostly complete with the CDM registry in place but not yet linked with several registries in Europe disallowing spot trading for many participants. As a result, price discovery is limited as the forward market is active but mostly on a principal-to-principal basis. However, a secondary market has emerged in Europe.

One of the most interesting features of the CDM is that, unlike the EU ETS, it is not restricted to industrial or energy emissions. It is therefore possible to carry out CDM projects in the domestic, transport or agricultural sectors and many such projects are under development. In this sense, it is possible to demonstrate that emissions trading as a concept can be inclusive and can cover every economic activity that has a substantive carbon footprint. The main variable is the carbon price which must be at a sufficiently high level to enable the abatement activity.

In conclusion, emissions trading is now a proven concept in relation both to achieving environmental policy aims and doing so with market mechanisms. This achievement has not gone unnoticed in North America, with international pressure building from all sides for linkage to be extended globally. This debate is being taken forward in the context of international negotiations to find a successor to the Kyoto Protocol. In addition, many market practitioners have decided to conclude transactions outside the formal compliance market, creating an exciting and innovative voluntary market which admits companies, countries or sectors currently excluded from the scope and mechanisms of the Kyoto Protocol, such as retail customers. The challenges of reaching a new global agreement among actors with vastly different political agendas cannot be overestimated but, with the science and impacts of climate change also globally understood and accepted, emissions trading provides an attractive financial toolbox to take climate change policy to the next stage.

Greg Dunne is a director and founding shareholder of ICECAP, one of the largest private sectors traders of emissions credits arising from the flexible mechanisms of the Kyoto Protocol. He is responsible for origination of emissions reduction projects throughout the world with a particular focus on Asia and South America. +44 (0)20 7340 0910 greg@icecapltd.com.

19 Greenhouse gas reporting

Standards for carbon disclosure are rising. Tom Woollard at
ERM discusses current reporting practices in giving a complete,
transparent picture.

When the first Carbon Disclosure Project (CDP) information request was
sent to the world's largest companies in May 2002, the vast majority of
businesses were only just beginning to appreciate the range of issues
presented by climate change. Five years on and with the publication of
Carbon Disclosure Project 5, more than 70% of companies contacted are
reporting emissions of carbon dioxide and other greenhouse gases – up
from under 50% in 2006. At the same time, climate change programmes
and climate change reporting have become important features of future
business strategy and risk management, as can be seen from the growing
number of climate change-related indices such as FTSE4Good, the Dow
Jones Sustainability Index and Ceres.

The uncertainty that incomplete, non-standardised and unverified carbon
disclosure generates can become another cause of unwanted share price
volatility and declining stakeholder confidence. Complete carbon disclosure, on the other hand, allows companies to distribute resources
effectively and permits investors to direct assets towards long-term, value-
creating companies. Transparency to stakeholders and the dialogue it
generates can also act as a means for identifying other areas for improving
business management and gives the company clues as to where to look
next for potential growth.

Complete disclosure on carbon related emissions also allows proactive
companies to showcase their strengths against less transparent competitors. Several multinationals have been quick to identify the importance
of climate change to the wider public and have gained significant reputation advantage by being seen as 'market leaders', in how they disclose
information to stakeholders on their carbon footprint and on the potential implications of climate change to their business. At this stage of the
debate, reputation advantage can be gained as much through effective

Reduction targets

While 32 out of the 50 companies presented quantified carbon reduction plans with defined timescales, the plans varied significantly in detail. Some websites gave a single one line reduction number whilst others provided detailed information by product, region and business area.

External verification

36 companies included some kind of verification statement although in most cases it was difficult to ascertain exactly what data had been verified. Many of the verification statements were unclear about the verification of carbon specific data.

Carbon intensity

Over half of the FTSE50 companies (26) gave information on carbon intensity with comparable data from past years.

Where intensity data was provided, in almost all cases historic or past information was used for comparison. Of the companies providing past data, 17 provided data going back to before 2005 but only 5 companies went back as far as 2000 or before. Carbon dioxide intensity information varied hugely. Metrics included CO_2 per £1m of turnover through to tonnes of CO_2 per employee, kilogram of CO_2e per tonne of finished product and some use their own intensity index unit. Most of this intensity information was only applicable to part of any one company's operations.

Survey conclusions

Most of the companies surveyed are undoubtedly feeling their way towards providing stakeholders with a more uniform approach to carbon emissions reporting via the web. The survey revealed that while most FTSE50 companies are still a long way from standardizing their carbon emissions reporting via the web, there has been some progress, particularly among companies which stick most closely to voluntary reporting guidelines such as those contained in the GHG Protocol Corporate Standard or the World Business Council for Sustainable Development Greenhouse Gas Protocol.

While the most successful reporters use voluntary guidelines, there remains a high degree of inconsistency in exactly what carbon emissions data is being reported, where it comes from and what it says about a company's current performance. The bar set by the FTSE4Good disclosure criteria is 'that companies disclose reliable, consistent and comparable data on GHG emissions.'

In the absence of regulatory requirements, the ERM survey highlights some of the baseline ingredients for effective web-based reporting in this area. It shows, for example, the importance of tabulating emissions data, indicating emissions sources and providing clear access to all relevant data. Companies may also win praise for illustrating their data with one or two eye catching graphics – a supermarket trolley, for example or an oil well to show carbon sources and reduction targets – and by ensuring that all terms are clearly explained.

In this, as in other areas, the web is an important window on the company and, in terms of carbon emissions disclosure, companies are having to rise to the challenge not only of providing the window, but also keeping it clean and allowing visitors to understand exactly what they are looking at. The move towards putting more standardized carbon emissions data on the web is an essential part of this process.

Good practice guidelines for public CO_2 reporting

The following paragraphs summarize good practice guidelines for the public reporting of CO_2 emission data. Carbon reporting should be done using the most standardised method for emissions accounting: The World Business Council for Sustainable Development and World Resources Institute (WBCSD/WRI) GHG protocol (corporate revised version). Direct and indirect emissions should be accounted for using the three 'Scopes' described in the GHG Protocol (See above table).

Emissions should be disclosed in absolute measures (assessing affects of carbon constraints) as well as indexed measures (for assessing different business units' performance, setting targets and benchmarking against other companies).

Where possible, indirect (Scope 3) emissions should be disclosed. Stakeholders are increasingly expecting corporations to report on the carbon footprint of their activities across the full life cycle. This can help them form a view on exposure to carbon risk through the supply chain or in the customer base.

Future emissions should be modelled as accurately as possible, balancing predicted growth with factors such as improvements in energy efficiency and purchased renewable/clean energy. A widespread problem with current emissions disclosure is the focus on historic performance, rather than future targets and expected implications.

The methodology for information collection should be consistent across all sites and should be described in detail as, even when working to standard protocols, variation in interpretation and results is still common place. Probable sources of error should be commented on and an estimate of their impact on the results should be given.

When providing carbon-related information on the web the following guidelines may be useful:

- **Clarity** – Be clear about exactly what you're reporting, what the emissions sources are and that the sums really do add up. An analyst who can't make the sub totals add up to an absolute total will quickly lose confidence in what is being reported. Avoid using jargon as far as possible and ensure you explain all specialist terms, possibly in the form of a glossary.

- **Signposting** – Use clear, unambiguous tabs and in some cases illustrative material to indicate core data and related contextual material. Try and group your carbon emissions data in one place, rather than have them dotted around the web site.

- **Use of graphics** – As in other areas of the web, graphics can be a powerful tool to explain data and trends. Think about the business you are in and whether a graphic could be used to link climate change performance with what you do (eg a retailer's use of a shopping trolley to show diminishing levels of carbon intensity).

- **Sources** – If you have more than one source of information on carbon emissions – eg a pdf and an html CSR report – make sure that different sources are consistent in terms of the information being presented. An interested party must be able to make the assumption that one web-based source is consistent with another.

- **Performance: past, present and future** – Remember that those using the web are frequently trying to make an initial assessment of performance. Where possible provide consistent carbon intensity data as well as absolute carbon emissions data. Also try and show how latest emissions data compares with past figures and set out clear reduction targets for the future. Are you leaving interested parties with a clear understanding of your intentions and your success to date in becoming a less carbon intense business?

- **The role of stakeholders** – Investors and other stakeholders have an important role to play in encouraging good practice via the web. With the prospect of a carbon constrained economy having an impact across all business sectors, stakeholders have a right to expect the availability of clear, consistent and, where appropriate, well illustrated carbon data on company websites. If web-based carbon data is in any way hard to find or confusing, a stakeholder should feed this message back to the company concerned.

While projects such as the Carbon Disclosure Project – currently backed by 315 of the world's largest investment houses with US$41 trillion under management – are raising the standard of carbon disclosure generally, it remains a priority for interested stakeholders and companies to ensure that carbon data are reported in a clear, consistent, accurate and standardized manner.

ERM's climate change and risk teams offer services to help clients answer the following questions:

- How will climate change impact my businesses?

- What are the key climate change threats?

- Where are the greatest climate change impacts?

- What is the likely magnitude of impact?

- What climate change mitigation and adaptation options should be considered?

Tom Woollard is a Principal Partner and member of the executive committe at ERM UK. Tom has been advising multinational corporations on a wide range of environmental and sustainability issues for the last 20 years.

Further details: www.erm.com

Sector	Number of Companies	Provide a total emissions figure (absolute)	Provide a total absolute figure comprising all the emissions disclosed on their website?	Units of absolute emissions disclosure	Data includes Scope 1	Data includes Scope 2	Data includes Scope 3	Disclose quantifiable targets for carbon emissions reduction	Provide quantifiable information regarding future financial commitment to carbon emissions reduction?	Report carbon intensity	Disclose historically comparable intensity data
Manufacturing	6	5	3	4 CO_2e, 1CO_2	5	5	2	4	1	1	1 of 1
Finance	13	5	5	1 CO_2e, 9CO_2	9	9	4	7	3	8	8 of 8
Retail & CG	12	11	9	7 CO_2e, 4CO_2	9	9	4	7	1	9	8 of 9
Media	7	5	4	1 CO_2e, 4CO_2	5	4	3	5	0	2	2 of 2
Resources	8	7	5	6 CO_2e, 1CO_2	7	6	4	6	4	3	3 of 3
Utilities	4	4	1	2 CO_2e, 2CO_2	3	3	2	3	0	4	4 of 4
Total	50	40	27	21 CO_2e, 21CO_2	38	36	19	32	9	27	26 of 27

Figure 1: Carbon reporting via the web: an ERM survey of FTSE 50 companies

20 The EU emissions trading scheme

By turning each tonne of CO_2 into a tradable commodity, the EU is hoping to create an incentive to reduce emissions. Caroline Austwick and Madlen King at Lloyd's Register ask, "but what are the risks?"

Around 12,000 sites across Europe are now involved in trading carbon dioxide (CO_2) – a new commodity that cannot be seen or touched but whose value has been worth from over €30 per tonne to as little as €0.03.

This relatively new market was created in 2005 by the European Union Emissions Trading Scheme (EU ETS) as part of Europe's strategy to reduce emissions in line with their overall Kyoto Protocol commitment – a 7.7% reduction in emissions from 1990 levels to be achieved by 2010.

It is the first scheme of its size and complexity aimed at reducing CO_2. Phase I runs from 2005 to 2007 and Phase II from 2008 to 2012. The time-frame for Phase III (2013 and beyond) is not yet set. Phase II will see the scheme expand to include new EU member countries and decisions made on proposals to include new sectors, such as aviation, and additional Greenhouse Gases.

The aim of the scheme, to reduce CO_2 emissions, is urgently required in the battle against global warming, but what are the key risks for businesses, Member States and others involved? Are companies in the EU ETS disadvantaged and how can participants minimise their risks?

This chapter examines the more significant risks for those in the EU ETS and how they can be mitigated. It draws mainly on experience from Phase I, but also looks forward to future risks under Phase II.

Brief introduction to the EU ETS

The EU ETS, referred to as a 'cap and trade' scheme, is designed to cost-effectively reduce CO_2 emissions in Europe. It differs from traditional mandatory methods of managing environmental issues, such as setting emission limits, through what are commonly called 'command and control' measures.

In essence it works like this:

Each country sets a total 'cap' on the CO_2 emissions from all the industries in the scheme.[1] The cap is calculated using a number of factors such as historical emissions from the industries included, the country's Kyoto target[2] and the estimated future emissions from the industries involved (potential growth rates).

Once approved by the European Commission (EC), the cap determines the number of 'allowances', also called EUAs (European Union Allowances), that each country can issue to their installations through a 'National Allocation Plan'.

Each allowance is equal to one tonne of CO_2 establishing a common 'currency' for trading.

So, for example, in the UK out of an annual cap of 215 million allowances in Phase I, around 205 million were issued to existing installations and 10 million were set aside for new ones.[3] In most cases, allowances were issued free of charge in yearly 'allocations' – but some (e.g. Ireland) auctioned a small percentage to recover their administration costs. The allowances given to each installation were listed in the country's allocation plan.

---

1. The scheme covers activities such as combustion plants over 20MW (e.g. power stations, boilers), steel works, cement manufacturing, pulp and paper plants, brickworks, ceramics production and oil refineries.

2. Typically targets are to reduce or stabilise emissions, but some countries were allowed to increase emissions.

3. This total does not include the allowances cancelled in the UK that were no longer needed for installations 'opted-out' of the scheme on the basis of existing requirements, such as those in the UK Emissions Trading Scheme and with Climate Change Agreements.

Every year an installation publicly reports its annual emissions (verified by an independent verification body) and 'surrenders' (gives back) the equivalent number of allowances. For example, an installation that receives 100,000 allowances and emits 110,000t CO_2 would surrender their 100,000 allowances issued from the government along with a further 10,000 allowances bought from the market (or possibly borrowed from their next year's allocation[4]).

Allocations and surrendering are done through an online registry where the operator's allowances are held in an account and can be transferred when bought and sold.

By turning each tonne of CO_2 into a tradable commodity, the EU hoped to stimulate investment in emissions reductions. Operators could recover the costs of any improvements through selling any allowances achieved to those less able to reduce their emissions. Unfortunately in Phase I too many allowances were issued compared with the actual emissions made. This resulted in the price of EUAs suddenly falling and thus the incentive to reduce emissions disappeared.[5]

Learning from Phase I, the EC has required countries to tighten their caps for Phase II (issue fewer allowances) and create 'scarcity' in the market to maintain a higher carbon price. This has established a higher price so far of around €20, but whether this will be maintained throughout Phase II as emissions are reported remains to be seen.

While this much-abbreviated description appears relatively straightforward, it is fair to say few companies and countries truly appreciated the complexity of what they were getting into and the potential risks involved.

---

4. Installations receive their next year's allocation before they have to surrender the previous year's allowances – so they can potentially borrow from one year to the next, but they risk running out of allowances in the last year of the Phase. Allowances cannot be 'carried over' from one Phase to the next.

5. This over-allocation in many countries was caused by several factors – countries were worried about the potential adverse effects on their industries and there was a lack of accurate historic emissions information on which to base the cap.

Risks for companies and installations

Each installation in the scheme requires a Greenhouse Gas Permit (GHG Permit) and must monitor and report CO_2 emissions in line with a 'monitoring and reporting plan' (M&R Plan) approved by the local competent authority or CA (such as the Environment Agency in the UK).

This sounds straightforward – so where is the risk?

Failing to obtain a permit

First, if an existing eligible installation has not obtained a GHG Permit (and should have done, i.e. it is not new), it faces enforcement action. At worst, it could be shut down and at best it will not receive any free allocation of allowances and therefore has to purchase them. The latter is because 'late comers' who do not feature into the country's allocation plan (approved on a specific date prior to commencement of the phase) do not qualify for their share of free allowances.[6] This is potentially costly, especially for any smaller installations that are simply not aware of the requirements.

Claiming ignorance of the legislation is no defence for failing to get a permit.

Risks such as these can be avoided by companies if they vigilantly review any changes to new legislation. In the UK for example, there is a new proposal known as the Carbon Reduction Commitment – this will affect a much larger number of companies, based on their electricity use. There are Government websites and industry liaison groups such as the International Emissions Trading Association (IETA) that provide useful information on developments such as these.

Incorrect monitoring and reporting

Second, operators risk monitoring and reporting their emissions incorrectly. M&R Plans, approved by the CA, set out how the installation must monitor and calculate its CO_2 emissions. For some, for example with one

---

6. The UK set up a 'missing installations' reserve for 'late entrants' so that they received some free allowances – but less than if they had been included in the NAP. Other countries did not set up such reserves.

gas boiler and one fuel source, these are relatively easy. For others, such as oil refineries with many emissions sources, the M&R Plan is complicated and requires significant resources. Missing out a decimal point or using a wrong emission factor can have a surprisingly large effect on a total emission result.

Under-reporting of emissions may incur legal action. On the other hand, over-reporting of emissions means operators surrender more allowances than they really need to – a potentially costly exercise depending on the overestimate.

Provision of sufficient resources for monitoring can be an issue within companies, since it may not be recognised as a priority. But with the potential penalties and risks involved, companies need to ensure that they include this in their risk management strategies and set aside sufficient resources.

To prevent mistakes in reporting, the EU ETS requires 'verification' by independent, accredited verifiers. Such organisations check that monitoring is performed in accordance with the approved plan, and that data and calculations do not contain errors (typically referred to as 'misstatements').

Robust verification of procedures and data can uncover problems within company reporting systems and detect errors that may otherwise be costly to the company. To reduce the risks, companies are beginning to understand that emissions' reporting is as important as financial reporting and are now applying the same rigor to its collection. Further risk management is obtained through the engagement of competent, fully accredited verifiers to ensure both the company and the CA can rely upon the emissions reported.

Deadlines

Third, significant risks surround meeting the numerous legislated deadlines. For example, failure to surrender the right number of verified allowances on time (30 April each year) results in a fine of €40 per allowance in Phase I, increasing to €100 per allowance in Phase II. The installation, in addition to this fine, then still has to obtain the allowances to surrender. Although some leniency was applied in the early years, several installations in the UK incurred these fines for not meeting the deadline.

Minimising non-compliance risk

In summary, to minimise the risks of incorrect monitoring and the resultant delays in verification and surrendering, operators must ensure that they:

- prepare for verification (have all information and data ready for the verifier);

- implement robust data management and quality assurance so that the information is free from misstatements;

- ensure the verifier is engaged early and is able to start work before the end of the year – (the period prior to surrender is extremely busy for verifiers); and

- discuss any monitoring and reporting problems with the CA as soon as they are identified – this can help avoid getting a 'non-verified' statement from the verifier (requiring the CA to then determine annual emissions).

Trading in a volatile market

Moving outside purely administrative and procedural risks are the risks involved with buying and selling allowances within a market of fluctuating prices.

For most, the goal is to sell allowances when the price is high and buy allowances when the price is low. However, in such an immature market with very little history to draw on that is heavily influenced by political decisions – it has been difficult to understand the key drivers and therefore to predict what would happen with the price. This showed clearly in 2006 when the price soared to €30 in early April and dropped dramatically in late April as soon as the market became aware that installations had emitted less than expected.[7]

---

7. See: http://www.defra.gov.uk/environment/climatechange/trading/eu/ results/pdf/carbon-summary.pdf

To minimise risks of price fluctuations it is advisable to watch the market, understand how the key factors influence the carbon price (such as gas and coal prices, power prices, government announcements, weather conditions, production rates) and seek advice from trading experts. Lessons from Phase I will undoubtedly be taken on board within Phase II both by analysts as well as operators.

Many of the larger industries have now assessed potential risks and put in place mechanisms to reduce their frequency and impacts. They actively engage in trading, not solely for compliance purposes but also seeking to profit. Gradually, as more industries learn about how trading works and how to minimise potential risks, some may also start looking for potential opportunities, instead of viewing the EU ETS as a purely regulatory imposition.

Competition risks

Installations were often grouped into 'industry sectors' and with regard to allocations were treated similarly within a country to reduce 'internal' competition issues. In other words, they generally received the same 'reduction or increase' in their allocation compared to their average historic emissions.

However, sectors were seldom treated equally by different countries throughout the EU. This potentially causes competition issues where sectors across Europe are competing in the same market. Sectors in countries that received fewer allowances potentially have to buy allowances originating from an installation in another country (possibly from the same sector) that had been issued with more than they required. This results in a transfer of wealth, but with no proper emissions reductions in return.

There are also risks for EU companies that do business in the global economy. Companies from outside Europe are not subject to the EU ETS, and therefore face the financial advantage of not having to purchase allowances if they increase their CO_2 emissions. Some industry groups are currently taking their government or the EC to court over Phase II

phases become more transparent, others should carefully examine the potential benefits.

The greatest opportunities lie in the financial rewards for reducing emissions and having allowances to sell. These may be very lucrative, particularly if carbon prices remain relatively high and if action is taken early in the next phase.[9]

But there are other advantages that should not be overlooked:

- **Reputation** – complying properly with the EU ETS is important for company reputations, incurring heavy EU ETS penalties would potentially undermine public confidence and trust in a large corporation.

- **Proving green credentials** – many companies are now committed to reducing their emissions and making 'carbon neutral' claims. Compliance with the EU ETS and achieving verified reductions at source makes an input to such commitments.

- **Additional savings** – reducing emissions from fuel use, not only frees up allowances to sell, but reduces fuel bills.

- **Improving communication** – with carbon trading placing assets and risks into company financial reports and in some cases influencing share prices, communication between finance directors and environmental managers is improving, potentially leading to greater opportunities for investment in reductions.

- **Future phases** – with auctioning set to play a greater role in future phases of the scheme, reducing emissions now will reduce the number of allowances a company may need to purchase in the future.

Of course, as far as climate change is concerned, the greatest opportunity is to prevent global warming and the greatest risk is from doing nothing at all.

---

9. Actions to reduce emissions and create allowances to sell early in Phase II will bring extra allowances to potentially sell each

Caroline Austwick is an environmental consultant for LRQA. She is the Director of Environmental Policy Solutions, an environmental consultancy offering specialist advice for business and government on carbon management and emissions trading, particularly the EU Emissions Trading Scheme. Contact: Caroline Austwick 07776 270 749 caroline.austwick@sky.com

Madlen King is the Greenhouse Gas Manager for LRQA, with global responsibility for all EU Emissions Trading Scheme (EUETS) and ISO 14064 verification services. She represents LRQA on the UK Emission Trading Group, liaising with both competent and regulatory authorities and having input into the guidance documents for such schemes. Madlen is participating in the contract for the European Commission to prepare the technical content of the Monitoring, Reporting and Verification Commission Decision for the inclusion of Aviation into the EU ETS. Contact: madlen.king@lrqa.com

LRQA, member of the Lloyd's Register Group, is a leading independent provider of Business Assurance services. Our climate change services include validation and verification of carbon inventories, footprint and project emissions, as well as CSR report assurance. Voluntary and regulated carbon market schemes we cover include ISO14064, Voluntary Carbon Standard (VCS 2007), regional schemes, and Kyoto Protocol mechanisms, Clean Development Mechanism (CDM), Joint Implementation (JI) and the EU Emissions Trading Scheme.

We have over 25 years of experience in assessment and certification of quality, environmental and health & safety management systems. Our clients include large global organisations, bringing transparency and recognised assurance to their business processes and systems.

Lloyd's Register is an independent risk management organisation that works to help improve its clients' quality, safety, environmental and business performance throughout the world, because life matters.

21 The voluntary carbon market

"How do you bring credibility and trust to the voluntary carbon market?", ask Dr. Anne-Marie Warris and Pem Charnley at Lloyd's Register.

In this chapter, we will be looking, with compelling evidence supplied from the first in-depth survey on the subject, at why there is such a strong need for a voluntary carbon standard to assure the voluntary carbon market.

The voluntary carbon market offers huge scope for the corporate sector, as well as individual buyers, especially if they are not part of a regulated market. For many players, the regulated carbon market often means delays and restrictions. What the regulated market *does* provide is a substantial level of assurance that emissions reductions are both real and measurable. The voluntary market must therefore, ensure that it can match these benefits.

For the voluntary carbon market to flourish and grow, it is essential that it is supported by a standard that provides buyers of carbon credits with trust and reassurance. Lack of credibility of some of the offset projects coming to the market has so far been the main drawback to what is surely a market that is not only growing dramatically, but promises to deliver far more in the near future.

In July 2007, Ecosystem Marketplace and New Carbon Finance released their comprehensive paper on the voluntary carbon market, entitled *State of the Voluntary Carbon Markets 2007: Picking Up Steam*. Over 70 organisations involved in all stages of the supply chain were surveyed, from developers through to retailers with the research covering five continents.

This exhaustive study of the market was seminal and brought to the public's attention many positives. Most importantly, the report declared that 2006 had seen the market grow by 200% and predicted that 2007 would see this trend continue. Despite such exponential growth, voluntary carbon trading still remains miniscule when compared to the different regulated markets around the globe. However, we should be concentrating, not on its current size, but on the opportunities it can provide.

But the report was admonitory also. It warned what others have already argued: that transparency within the voluntary market is imperative if it is to enjoy credibility.

As stated, the 200% growth in the market is certainly positive. Proposed market entrants include leading brands such as Dell, Yahoo!, Google, BP and Nike, who have all announced their desire for business sustainability.

Yahoo!, for example, has announced that they "are changing [their] energy consumption practices as well as investing in greenhouse gas reduction projects to make [their] impact on the climate essentially neutral." Clearly then, big businesses are taking notice and the voluntary carbon market continues to become big business as a result.

As the report states, the voluntary markets denote a demand by businesses for action on carbon emissions. According to the companies surveyed, their desire for participation in the voluntary carbon market has centred on their corporate social responsibility (CSR) aims and a desire for credible 'green' credentials.

Innovation

The main reason for such rapid growth in the voluntary carbon market is its lack of regulation. This is a double-edged sword, credibility-wise, as we shall see, yet the lack of governmental intervention, per se, is what makes the voluntary carbon market so attractive.

Free from the shackles of bureaucracy and large transaction costs, flexibility becomes the key. Dr. Sally Uren, Director, Forum for the Future, said:

> "What happens in the voluntary market is that you get a lot of innovation and a lot of carbon offset projects that give you huge amounts of additionality in terms of wider sustainability benefits."

The market is thriving in those areas where the regulatory market has yet to become firmly established. 68% of customers are based in the US (understandably, as the US has not signed the Kyoto Protocol), and the percentage of projects being carried out in Africa is double that of the percentage of Clean Development Mechanism (CDM) projects in Africa. The overwhelming majority of CDM projects are being delivered in China and India. The survey went on to add that voluntary carbon markets serve as sources of experimentation, and, as with the example of Africa, are the most likely to reach poorer and smaller communities in developing countries.

One universally accepted standard

Lack of regulation can cause reservations amongst buyers of carbon credits, be they customers or organisations. How can they know for certain that their decision to run a business in a sustainable manner, to offset any remaining carbon emissions and adopt a carbon neutral approach can be assured without credible standards in place? A company's decision to offset carbon after it has reduced its carbon footprint as far as possible can only be positive, but what sort of offset does the company purchase and how can it assure that these offsets are genuine?

This is concurrent with the survey, which says that "the flexibility of the voluntary markets is both a source of strength and a weakness." Low transaction costs exist because no evidence is required of the quality of the offsets, as would be in a regulated market. The costs may indeed be minimal, yet customers are left unsure as to the real quality of the offsets purchased.

With the voluntary carbon market set to boom, it is vital that trust be brought to the forefront. So what measures have been taken to bring confidence to the market and what does the future hold, as corporations seek to continue their aim to achieve sustainability as committed to in their CSR aims? The only way to assure consumers, businesses and governments that the voluntary market is transparent and credible is through the development and implementation of a voluntary carbon standard that can be applied globally. The emission reductions must be real, measurable, permanent, additional and conservative. The standard needs to offer credible assurance in the form of validation and verification. It must also provide transparency in the form of a register which ensures carbon units are not double counted.

The options

Currently, there are two standards that have been accepted in the global marketplace: the Voluntary Carbon Standard 2007 (VCS 2007) and the Gold Standard. Both of these standards have been developed through consultation with industry experts, businesses and environmental experts. The three key criteria that both have met to offer added value to corporations and individuals looking to the voluntary carbon market as an alternative to the regulated carbon market are to:

- ensure the project emission reductions are real, measurable, permanent, conservative and additional;

- provide for controls to avoid duplicate claims through a number of GHG programmes via a registry;

- provide the credibility that independent third-party validation and verification offers.

VCS 2007

In 2005, The Climate Group (TCG), the International Emissions Trading Association (IETA), World Business Council for Sustainable Development (WBCSD) and the World Economic Forum (WEF) began working on developing a universally accepted voluntary carbon standard. The VCS version 1 was set up to try and deal with the issues of credibility, transparency and reliability, but it was a first draft of the standard. While it was used in the market right from the start, it was identified that a wider consultation with stakeholders as well as a credible registry system was needed to make the standard robust and globally accepted.

In November 2007, after consultation with over 1,000 stakeholders, IETA, the TCG and WBCSD launched VCS 2007[1]. The VCS Steering Committee, based on an agreement with the International Standards Organisation (ISO), has adapted portions of ISO 14064, the globally accepted greenhouse gas

---

1. Disclosure: Dr Anne-Marie Warris was retained to write the VCS 2007 based on the work of the VCS Steering Committee.

(GHG) standard for quantification and reporting of GHG and its validation and verification. Part 2 of ISO 14064 is used directly in the VCS 2007 and both 14064 Part 2, 14064 Part 3 and 14065 are used as reference documents.

The VCS 2007 meets and exceeds the needs of the voluntary carbon market by:

- providing transparency and credibility to the voluntary carbon market;

- being a rigorous global, base level standard for voluntary emission reductions and removals;

- creating a trusted and exchangeable voluntary emissions reduction/removal credit;

- allowing experimentation while stimulating innovation in GHG mitigation technologies;

- providing a secure, custodial service that offers assurance against double counting and provides transparency to the public;

- providing confidence that voluntary emission reductions/removals that are purchased are real, additional and permanent.

The VCS 2007 is overseen by an independent non-profit association with its own independent board. Projects validated against VCS version 1 will be grandfathered into VCS 2007.

"The VCS 2007 represents the consensus of key stakeholders and we hope that it will provide confidence and integrity in the rapidly growing VC market," said Andrei Marcu, President of IETA. "It is a much needed development that we hope will address concerns raised about the lack of oversight in this market segment."

Mark Kenber, Policy Director of The Climate Group, added, "All the stakeholders in the emerging voluntary carbon market recognise that standards are critical. Our Voluntary Carbon Standard introduces a stringent quality assurance to the market and underpins consumer confidence, market credibility and innovation in low carbon technologies."

Eron Bloomgarden, EcoSecurities US Country Director, said, "Continued development of stringent industry protocols, like the Voluntary Carbon Standard, will perhaps play the largest role in the continued maturation of the voluntary market, more so than legislation, education, or increased supply."

Main components of the VCS 2007

VCS 2007 is applicable to all projects in all jurisdictions. Its principles demand that transactions are measurable, permanent, additional, independently verified, and not double counted. In addition to baseline setting, projects must go beyond legal requirements including one of three tests, i.e. additionality is required.

Procedures, methodologies and credits from other credible GHG project programmes can be accepted when they have been confirmed as meeting the VCS 2007 requirements as a minimum, via a gap analysis.

Project developers can introduce new methodologies, developed outside any existing or not approved GHG programme. Such new methodologies will need to be double approved, e.g. confirmed by two independent bodies that the new methodology meets the requirements of the VCS 2007.

Validation and verification must be performed by organisations accredited by a member of the International Accreditation Forum, using ISO 14065 or by a VCS approved GHG programme. All Voluntary Carbon Units (VCU's) must be held in a VCS approved registry, providing assurance against double counting and double trading of carbon credits

Gold Standard

Gold Standard is, since early 2005, a separate organisation that is hosted by Basel Agency for Sustainable Energy (BASE), which is a United Nations Environment Programme (UNEP) collaborating centre.

The Gold Standard was initialised by the Worldwide Fund for Nature (WWF) in response to the concerns of individuals, academics and non-governmental organisations (NGOs), who felt that then-existing emission reduction projects were not lowering CO_2 levels to a degree they felt was urgently needed.

The standard evolved over a two-year period of direct consultation that was designed to ensure input was included from as wide a range of stakeholders as possible. Key players in the carbon market were consulted.

It offers a quality label to CDM/Joint Implementation (JI) and voluntary offset projects, fetching premium prices. Renewable energy and energy efficiency projects with sustainable development benefits are eligible. The Gold Standard is endorsed by over 44 NGOs worldwide and is preferred by a range of government and private actors.

It is not a stand-alone standard for offsets but provides an additional 'filter' for carbon offset buyers, allowing them to pick projects with higher sustainability credentials than other projects (all CDM/JI and VCS projects have to meet sustainability criteria).

Conclusion

The VCS 2007 is a credible means for businesses, organisations and individuals to reduce and offset their carbon emissions and it will prove to be an invaluable tool in helping businesses prove that their CSR aims and green 'credentials' can be trusted.

This, in turn, enhances the growth of a credible voluntary global carbon market that can spearhead both innovation and transparency, further educating consumers and businesses of the dangers of climate change, leading to measurable steps by us all to reduce our carbon emissions.

Sources:

http://www.brand.yahoo.com/forgood/environment/carbon_neutral.html

http://www.businessassurance.com/voluntary-carbon-standard/

http://www.ecosystemmarketplace.com/pages/article.news.php?component_id=5107&component_version_id=7497&language_id=12

www.v-c-s.org

http://www.cdmgoldstandard.org/

of oil, the only driver for the technology is climate change mitigation. As such, it is strongly dependent on the setting of a price for carbon emitted (or in this case, the reciprocal reward for not emitting). Such incentives may be set by tax or emissions trading schemes, although as we will outline below, such an incentive is not on offer. Other hurdles must be overcome before widespread deployment of the technology, including improving overall efficiency of the technology, creating legal and regulatory systems to ensure safe and effective deployment, and introducing systems to handle long-term liability and assurance of permanent storage.

Incentivising CCS

As indicated above, climate change mitigation is the only real driver for CCS technology development and deployment. Whilst enhanced oil recovery (EOR) using fossil CO_2 is possible, from an engineering and health and safety perspective, its application in many parts of the world is complicated, especially when attempted offshore. Consequently, EOR does not always present an immediate opportunity to monetise stored carbon at positive cost for private business. Moreover, it is dependent on proximity of CO_2 sources to oil fields amendable to CO_2 flooding.

In terms of storing CO_2, mitigating climate change is a public good that should ultimately be compensated for through appropriate fiscal and regulatory incentives. There are several means of doing this: taxing emissions so it is cheaper to store the CO_2 than emit (this works in Norway for Statoil's Sleipner project, where 1 million tonnes of CO_2 a year are injected into the sea-bed under the North Sea to avoid the county's CO_2 tax); develop cap-and-trade emissions programmes that recognise stored CO_2 as non-emitted, thus removing the obligation of those regulated to surrender units for CO_2 that was generated but stored (e.g. in the EU's greenhouse gas emissions trading scheme; EU ETS); allow project-based mechanisms to recognise CO_2 as an emission reduction against a baseline; offer other forms of financial incentives linked to products generated from sources employing CCS (e.g. feed-in tariffs for electricity generated from CCS fitted power plants); mandate the use of CCS for certain sources; or offer direct government subsidies to cover the CCS installation cost.

Of greatest interest in this context is the use of emissions trading schemes, as these are the chosen policy mechanism to regulate global greenhouse gas emissions (as laid out in the Kyoto Protocol). In this respect, there are currently several schemes, including the EU's ETS, the Kyoto Protocol's clean development mechanism (CDM) and joint implementation (JI) and other proposals for trading schemes in California and Australia. However, none of these formally recognise CCS projects as non-emissions or as a means of generating emissions reductions[2]. Work is currently underway to see how CCS projects can be included in both the EU ETS and the CDM.

In the case of EU ETS, work is currently going to look at how early projects could be 'opted-in' to Phase II (2008-12), after which the European Commission hopes to have fully reviewed the role of CCS and put in place an appropriate legal and incentives framework for the technology. With regard to the latter, this is underway at the time of writing and is coupled with a full review of the EU ETS for Phase III (2012+), and ultimately recognition for potential projects.

For the CDM, effort has been made to develop an acceptable accounting procedure[3] but there are outstanding questions regarding eligibility and concerns over the regulatory and legal structures for developing economies.

The immediate major stumbling block for incentivising CCS activities remains the challenging of dealing with the *permanence* of emission reductions achieved. Essentially, this revolves around the issues of good site selection, operation, management and closure in order to deliver a permanent emission reduction. The basis for this lies in the belief that the evolution of an appropriate regulatory scheme should ensure that potentially leaky sites are not selected in the first place. That said, there remains a need to allocate liability and create obligations for remediation, just in case one or two bad sites do slip through the net.

---

2 Although it is likely that AAUs may be traded from 2008 for CCS projects, as Norway already reports Sleipner as non-emission in its national greenhouse gas inventory

3 See IEA Greenhouse Gas R&D Programme (IEA GHG) ERM – Carbon Dioxide Capture and Storage: in the CDM. 2007/TR2, Cheltenham, April 2007.

In terms of guidance, several approaches are outlined in semi-binding regulatory texts, among them the IPCC 2006 guidelines. These form an important precedent, as this is the approach governments will adopt for reporting national emissions under the Kyoto Protocol compliance regime[5]. The guidelines outline a form of *de facto* regulatory approach by indicating a requirement for appropriate site selection, risk assessment, and monitoring of storage sites. They include an Annex outlining a range of possible techniques which can be applied in order to both detect the presence of CO_2 in target formations and monitor for CO_2 leaks into surrounding areas), the displacement of incumbent formation fluids and leakages at the surface (either the seabed or on land).

Despite the ongoing evolution of regulatory and legal frameworks for CCS, the sharing of long-term liability between the facility owners/operators and host countries remain largely unresolved. This said, it is widely acknowledged by policy-makers that there is a need to absolve the operator of liability for the site at some point after closure, depending on the operator providing demonstrable evidence of the likelihood of long-term secure storage of the CO_2.

Next steps...

Industry and governments both have key roles to play in realising the full potential of CCS. Industry can provide the capital, innovation and know-how needed to develop successful large-scale projects, while governments can provide the long-term policy and regulatory framework enabling widespread deployment of CCS on a commercial basis. This could be achieved through the development of more robust emissions trading schemes – for example, with a carbon price reflecting economy-wide abatement cost of the effort needed to stabilise atmospheric CO_2 concentrations. Ultimately, the public must also be convinced that the technology is needed, that it is safe, and that there are regulations in place to safeguard their health, environment and property.

---

5 Although the Kyoto Compliance for the current period 2008-12 is based on the IPCC 1996 Guidelines, which do not include specific guidelines for reporting emissions (and reductions) linked to CCS.

Uncertainty over CCS is primarily being driven by lack of clarity around what regimes might be in place in coming years to manage greenhouse gas emissions, at what sort of level, and at what sort of cost. As a result, while there is much research to improve technological understanding, create appropriate incentives and have enabling legal frameworks for CCS this writer senses that many potential developers and investors remain somewhat more circumspect than they might appear. Evidence for this can be found in BP's recent decision to terminate the DF1 project in Scotland. This came in spite of BP having spent considerable sums of money and intellectual capital trying to get the project off the ground.

Looking ahead, investors need clearer signals regarding the upside from CCS, prior to going ahead with planned projects. Clearly, as the world waits to see how a new regulatory and carbon cutting regime shapes up post Bali, there will be continuing debate over what constitutes effective CCS – from both the technology and regulatory perspective. However long it takes the politicians to come to terms with the reality of climate change, it is clear that CCS offers workable short-term solutions.

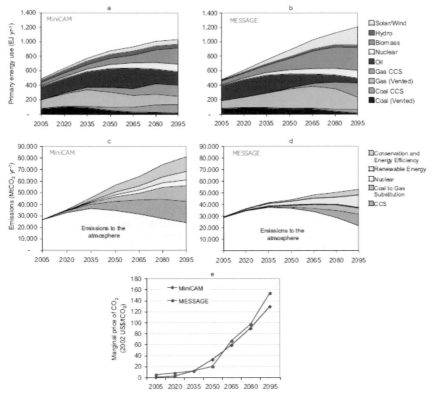

Figure 1: Future scenarios: using CCS to reduce carbon emissions

Source: IPCC Special Report on CCS, 2005

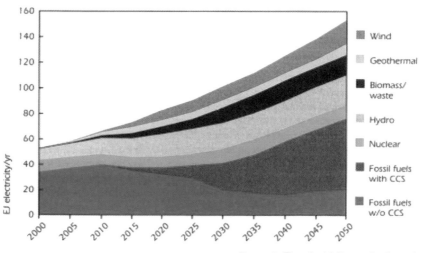

Figure 2: The electricity production mix

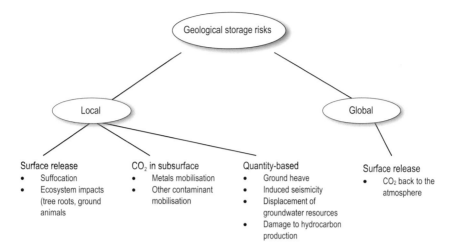

Figure 3: Taxonomy of possible risks of geological storage

Source: Wilson, E., and D. Keith. Geologic Carbon Storage: Understanding the Rules of the Underground. In Gale, J and Y. Kaya (eds). Proc. Of the 6th Int Conf. on Greenhouse Gas Control Techs (Vol I). October, 2003. Pergamon

Part 5

Energy use

23 Renewable energy in business

"A target of 15-16 per cent for renewables in total energy use has far-reaching implications for all types of organisation, not just energy suppliers", says Philip Wolfe, Executive Director of the Renewable Energy Association.

Energy supply has traditionally been a specialised business monopolised by a select few companies and treated at arm's length by consumers and corporate users alike. Are the threats of climate change and energy security, and the opportunities of new technology and decentralisation now going to change all that?

On the political stage, the European Union has signed up to a highly ambitious package of targets on emissions reductions, energy conservation and sustainable energy generation. At the corporate level progressive businesses of all sizes are recognising the financial and marketing benefits of a more enlightened approach to energy and other social and environmental issues.

The policy agenda, at least here in the UK, is some way from harmonising these two effects, but the drivers for accelerating deployment of renewable energy in particular are irresistible.

Emissions reductions	Binding
20% if unilateral, or	
30% if other developed nations join in	
Energy conservation	Non-binding
20% below current projections	
Renewables	Binding
20% of total energy	
10% of transport fuels	

First – the politics

The energy targets shown here are totals for the EU. At the time of writing, the national targets are unconfirmed, but the UK renewables target is likely to be 15-16% of total energy.

The target for renewables in *total energy* is novel. Historically the UK has focussed sustainable energy policy solely on the electricity sector, largely forgetting heat and transport energy. We have a 2020 'aspiration' to achieve 20% of electricity output from renewables (up from approaching 5% today), so some observers thought at first that we had the EU commitment already covered. Not so – electricity is less than one third of our total energy. Therefore, we'd need to generate over half of our electricity from renewables to reach 20% of total energy, if we continued to ignore heat and transport fuels.

At the level of total energy our task is all the more pressing. The UK achieves about 1.7% from renewables so we have little over a decade to increase this by an order of magnitude.

This creates the imperative, not just to do more of the same, but also to take action in some of the sectors that have previously been overlooked. In particular it will mean deploying renewables outside the traditional energy sector. This offers many opportunities to a wide range of corporate players – and many are already exploring their options.

Next – the customer

Consumers, like governments, are struggling to come to terms with the need to reduce emissions, while maintaining lifestyle. In particular, many are unsure of the contribution they can personally make. This means that most expect governments and businesses to take the lead.

The purchase of energy on so-called 'green tariffs' has been the obvious first step into renewables, but many are confused about the different options and the practical benefit they deliver.

There has also been a dramatic acceleration in the numbers of people installing renewable energy in their own homes. The added attraction of selling power back to the energy supplier is seen as a bonus.

And third – the response of business

Industry can benefit from any emerging business driver, if it reads the market and identifies a viable commercial response. Huge numbers of companies from outside the energy sector are now looking for ways of engaging with renewables.

Again this can start with the fairly passive purchase of green tariff energy. In practice this has questionable value in actually increasing the level of carbon-free capacity, as most renewable electricity is generated to meet suppliers' requirements under the Renewables Obligation (see below). This has also led to the perverse outcome that merchant renewable electricity is not treated as carbon free for the purposes of the Carbon Reduction Commitment, but as if it were fossil fuel generated!

Although this government 'policy accounting' issue needs resolving, the upside is that companies are looking to install their own portfolios of renewables. This includes photovoltaic roofs on warehouses, anaerobic digesters on farms, solar cooling in supermarkets and wind turbines for factories.

The great thing about renewables for businesses, and other users, is that it can provide energy at the point of use, and the wide range of options enables a match for almost any application. The Renewable Energy Association has had such a flurry of interest that it has set up a Users and Retailers Group to provide an interchange of ideas.

What every business can do

Of course, businesses and consumers alike can and should increase the sustainability of their energy supplies. This means improving the efficiency of their energy consumption, both through less wasteful usage and more efficient devices. Then they should find renewable sources for the unavoidable energy consumption they are left with.

There is a wide range of different renewable energy sources that can be used – the most suitable will depend on location, usage (and budget).

The most straightforward replacement for a gas or oil-powered heating system is a biomass boiler, where there are different options for fuels such as wood chips, pellets, solid wood and several fuel options. Biomass CHP units are now also becoming available, capable of producing power as well as heat. The main issues in selecting these products are siting, fuel storage and availability. Similar units powered by liquid biofuels or by biogas are also coming to the market.

But there are also options that produce energy directly from renewable sources. For electricity, the most common are wind, solar photovoltaics and hydropower. A primary factor in choosing these options is the availability of the energy resource – locality to a river or stream, southerly roof and façade area local wind speeds etc.

There are also a number of elemental heat sources, of which the most common are solar heating panels and various types of heat pump, which collect and amplify heat from the ground or the ambient air.

Individuals and companies wishing to pursue these options can get advice from the Energy Saving Trust, Carbon Trust or a variety of other services.

To help assess the more specific opportunities available, we now review the application areas, and some of the developments that will be needed for a tenfold growth in just twelve years.

Renewable energy policy measures

Successive Energy Reviews and White Papers have highlighted the need for increased contributions from renewables, and some policy measures have already been implemented. In addition to the emerging carbon market under the EUETS, the main renewables focussed mechanisms are:

- The Renewables Obligation (a misnomer; it should be the Renewable Electricity Obligation) sets a requirement for electricity suppliers to meet a part of their sales from renewables or pay a buy-out penalty.

- A Renewable Transport Fuels Obligation is to be introduced in April, designed to achieve a similar uptake of biofuels in the petrol and diesel markets. The quota has initially been set at 5% by volume in 2010.

- Two measures should lead to a small contribution for renewables in the building sector. Firstly, the Government has announced that all new homes must be zero carbon from 2016. Secondly, the Energy Efficiency Commitment is being extended to include some modest incentives for renewables.

- Finally, the Carbon Reduction Commitment will impose obligations on major corporates and this too could provide a driver for renewables (provided it is changed!)

The recent Energy White Paper acknowledges that current measures should take us to perhaps 5% of total energy from renewables by 2020. So we've got about one third of the new commitment covered – and that depends on the White Paper measures actually working to remove barriers and provide effective investment incentives.

Where might the other two-thirds come from?

Fortunately there are lots of possibilities – and we will need to use a broad portfolio of approaches to achieve the scale of change required. Let no one convince you there is a single easy answer.

New opportunities in the energy sector

Of course there is still plenty of potential, so before moving on to look at the less traditional areas here is a digest of the main opportunities:

- Large scale combined heat and power: the UK's historical focus on electricity has meant that heat – even heat used for power generation – has been neglected. Power stations typically waste perhaps 65% of their energy input. This is unacceptable in an energy constrained world, so new thermal generators should be located where the heat can be captured and used through combined heat and power (CHP). This is likely to mean more, but smaller power stations.

- The Biomass Task Force concluded that 7% of the UK's heat energy could come from biomass so some of our CHP generation can use renewable fuels.

- Thirdly, we can afford to be more ambitious with the Renewables Obligation. The industry proposes that the 2020 quota should be raised from the 20% specified in the Energy White Paper to 25-30%.

- Next there are other large renewable generation opportunities, which we can no longer afford to dismiss. Potential local environmental impacts have historically inhibited renewable projects, such as tidal barrages and hydropower stations. The Severn Tidal Barrage project, for example, could deliver 5% of our electricity. New approaches such as tidal lagoons might provide an alternative way of harnessing this energy resource. Similarly, the residual large hydro potential, mainly in Scotland, also needs to be reassessed.

- Furthermore, there need to be better measures to bring forward innovative generation technologies, especially tidal stream and wave power, where the UK leads the world.

- The UK is more limited in the likely penetration of bio-fuels owing to our lower land area in relation to population. Nonetheless, we should be capable of achieving the EU mandatory target of a 10% penetration of renewable fuels by 2020.

- The Renewable Transport Fuels Obligation (RTFO) will be met primarily by fuel providers 'blending in' the required percentage of bio-fuels into petrol and diesel. We must also encourage the development of 'high blend' fuels and the flex-fuel vehicles, which use them.

New opportunities in other sectors

The highest contribution to the missing two-thirds of new renewables contribution may actually come from today's poor relation – on-site power, especially heat. Our buildings must be made far more energy efficient and can then get most of their energy from on-site renewables such as solar heating, ground and air-source heat pumps, photovoltaics, biomass and pellet boilers or CHP, wind turbines and even small hydro stations.

The industry proposes several measures to massively increase the contribution of on-site renewables:

- The new Code for Sustainable Homes (CSH) needs to be adopted as a mandatory, rather than voluntary standard. The Code sets out various levels of energy sustainability, of which the top is Level 6 – zero carbon. So Building Regulations should be amended by 2016 to make CSH Level 6 a requirement.

- As interim measures to encourage energy efficiency and onsite renewables, the 2010 Building Regulations revision should require CSH Level 4 and the 2013 revision CSH Level 5.

- Similarly, we need measures for non-residential buildings. Government should introduce a Code for Sustainable Buildings and again use this as the basis for Building Regulations.

- But Building Regulations address only new construction and alterations. We need also to improve the 25 million homes already built. We propose an active programme to retrofit these buildings with energy efficiency and renewables, so they can progressively be raised to zero carbon standards, too. The programme may take two or three decades, but this still represents hundreds of thousand of properties each year.

- Much can also be achieved by positive planning policies of individual local authorities, such as the pioneering measures first adopted in Merton.

- Another area of great potential is the use of biomass residues and wastes converted by anaerobic digestion (AD), or similar processes, to biogas and fertiliser. The installation of AD plant on a significant proportion of our 300,000 farms can make a substantial contribution to the renewable energy target, either on-site or by feeding bio-methane into the gas network.

Where does the money come from?

Consumers would fund many of these measures through slightly higher energy prices. This is a sensible investment in a sustainable energy future. It also represents an overdue adjustment for the artificially low prices, which have contributed to our damaging profligacy in recent decades.

Cash raised from climate change related taxation, such as the Fossil Fuel Levy surplus, auctions of carbon allowances under the EUETS and air transport duty, can comfortably cover whatever part would need to come from the Treasury. It is only right that such 'polluter pays' measures should be redirected to clean energy sources.

The Stern Report showed why any such financial costs need to be seen as comparative rather than absolute, and suggested that the overall cost of climate change mitigation should be roughly 1% of GDP. The raft of measures proposed here would require only a small fraction of this.

Philip Wolfe has over 30 years' experience in the renewable energy industry. He is the current Executive Director of the Renewable Energy Association, the representative body for the UK renewables industry across all sectors and technologies.

24 Enterprise energy and carbon reduction

"How do you manage the operational and financial risks in energy procurement, while making a real impact on greenhouse emissions?", asks Peter Webster, Director of Utilyx Climate Change Group.

In January 2008 EU President Jose Manuel Barosso announced ambitious plans to tackle climate change across European economic member states by reducing greenhouse emissions by 20% by 2020. The President claimed this 'historic' announcement would result in 'the first economy of the low-carbon age' – and even suggested that reductions could rise to 30% if supported by a global deal. While some observers have claimed the 20% reduction plan was ambitious, others have said it is simply not possible.

One thing, on which business leaders, politicians and analysts are agreed however, is that the plan will have a wide-ranging impact on their businesses over the next decade. Reducing greenhouse gas emissions and more efficient energy consumption go hand in glove.

Philanthropy or profitability – that is the question?!

While it would be great to think that much of these reductions will be achieved by business leaders' desire to save the planet, much will be the result of a desire to save money. New Legislation will force businesses to introduce new environmentally friendly practices and the threat of rising costs, such as the UK's Carbon Reduction Commitment scheme, Phase two of the EU Emissions Trading Scheme (ETS), and large fines coupled with the rising costs of energy will likely be the number one driver for businesses to 'go green'.

We have already seen a rush by many leading global organisations to implement climate change initiatives that have reduced exposure to volatile energy prices and improved the company's green credentials. Many of the early adopters have been accused of 'green washing' – implementing so-called climate change programmes that are more about perception than reality.

Cause and effect

So, how does a company go about reducing the operational and financial risks associated with energy procurement, while making a positive (and real) impact on greenhouse emissions?

The first phase of implementing any energy efficiency and carbon reduction strategy is to understand the main causes of carbon emission within a business. 40% of energy consumed in the UK is used in buildings – this is mainly for heating and air conditioning or, in the case of food retailing, for refrigeration. A significant amount of this energy is wasted at the point of conversion (in boilers or air-conditioning units) and through energy inefficient buildings.

Conducting an energy and carbon audit will tell you where the majority of your energy is being used, whether savings can be made by refining the process or upgrading the technology used, and where the energy and climate change costs are within the business. This audit can be conducted internally, or in conjunction with an energy and climate change risk consultancy, but it forms an integral part of an energy management and reduction plan.

Once the audit has been completed a tool known as a carbon abatement curve can be used to enable a company to decide what options are open to them to reduce energy costs and carbon emissions. The carbon abatement curve plots a series of measures against their respective cost, how much carbon it will save and, in combination with effective energy management, it will enable businesses to identify the things they can do to abate or displace emissions. The curve will also identify how the attainment of these goals can be achieved by energy efficiency initiatives or by changing energy source (oil to gas, coal to clean coal, heating oil to biofuel, etc.).

Modern Building Automation Systems are sophisticated computer-based arrangements, monitoring and controlling temperature and other sensors throughout a single corporate headquarters building. They can improve working conditions and save a considerable amount of energy, often by simple measures such as switching off lights when rooms are not occupied.

Companies have been slow to install BAS systems, particularly where they lease the buildings. Higher electricity costs and future charges for carbon emissions give everyone a big incentive to upgrade the buildings that they occupy, and will make energy-efficient and automated buildings more attractive, commanding higher rents.

Using an energy and climate change audit can reduce energy consumption, carbon emissions and cost to the business.

Profitable investments

One of the biggest misconceptions about implementing energy reduction and climate change projects is that they cost money. While some initiatives do have a cost on bottom line profitability or top line growth, there are a large number of things that don't cost the business anything. Investments in insulation and solar heating, for example, can be profitable ones because they reduce energy consumption, remove some of the businesses' exposure to consumption and price risk, and reduce carbon emissions.

One large UK retailer, has developed a novel initiative to encourage its employees to turn off lights when they left meeting rooms, shut down electrical equipment rather than leave them on standby and to reduce excess office heating/cooling/re-heating. Faced with increasing energy costs year-on-year and aggressive energy and carbon reduction targets the company has put up stickers around the building that make a simple, but effective point reminding staff 'every time you leave the lights on you are burning your bonus!!'. Energy consumption in the company has fallen as a result.

Implementation issues

Once a series of energy efficiency and climate change projects have been identified by the audit, a business must look at the issues of implementing it across the entire organisation. Do working practices need to be reengineered? Does there need to be investment in new technologies – and if so, which? Is there a need for a new energy and climate change policy to be drawn up to provide guidelines on energy procurement (buying green rather than brown) and set triggers that ensure sufficient supply is purchased to ensure business as usual, but protects the organisation from price shocks? If the business did switch from one type of fuel to another what would the investment need to be (considering that if you switch to a cleaner fuel, you may have to invest in new boilers, heating and cooling systems and fuel storage)?

One project that is currently delivering real results with a number of the UK's leading supermarket chains is a replacement of all fresh produce refrigeration cabinets once the existing units reach end of life, or when stores are opened or refitted. Not only are the refrigeration units more energy efficient, they also have in-built management systems that enable them to power down once they reach a defined temperature, but power up when temperatures rise to a pre-destined level to ensure food safety.

Budget constraints are no longer a barrier to energy efficient projects. Equipment suppliers are keen to lease their plant on shared-saving schemes. Investors looking to benefit from tax incentives on renewable projects are keen to invest – selling heat or power on very competitive terms. Businesses with money to invest in energy efficiency and renewable projects can obtain generous grants and loans from government sources.

No magic bullet!

The most important thing to remember for companies looking to implement energy management and climate change projects is that there is no magic bullet; no one size fits all initiative that will improve green credentials and add value to the business. What is certain is that climate change will become an increasingly important issue on the corporate agenda and energy management will become the mantra of almost every organisation.

How do we know this? Because it has already started – and the companies that will make the most of the opportunities to reduce energy consumption and reduce the amount of carbon it emits are not necessarily the ones being trumpeted in the pages of the business media. The companies that are already seeing the benefits of climate change initiatives are the ones that have undertaken the research, considered their options and selected the most appropriate ones for their business.

Carbon futures

Large energy users are already required to participate in the European Emissions Trading System (EU-ETS). This sets targets for carbon emissions reductions, and requires participants to buy certificates (called EUAs) to offset any excess CO_2 production. The EUAs are freely traded. At the end of phase 1, which ended last year, EUAs traded for a few cents – there were plenty to go around. Phase 2, covering the next 3 years has already started strongly, trading at around €20/tonne of carbon. Phase 3 looks like being a lot tighter, with potentially higher prices. The Stern report suggested that the price should be $85/tonne.

The EU-ETS has become the marker for carbon costs, with governments keen to draw more and more businesses into some form of carbon trading. Meanwhile, the option of voluntarily offsetting your carbon will become increasingly expensive.

Most significantly, all electricity generators are part of the EU-ETS, and have to buy EUAs to match their CO_2 production. Their costs are passed straight through to customers – the recent sharp rise in power prices is directly linked to the cost of carbon. A third of the cost of wholesale electricity is now made up of the carbon price.

A change of climate

What is clear is that energy and carbon reduction will continue to be a significant issue for business leaders throughout the next decade. The imperative will be to develop long-term carbon reduction and renewables strategies that deliver benefits to both the environment and the business alike, rather than the high rhetoric but low content expressions of intent we have seen from some in recent years. Only then will businesses start to make a real contribution to slowing the rate of climate change.

Businesses that fail to do so will, very quickly, start to see the costs rise exponentially and their profits (and stock prices) fall significantly!

Peter Webster has worked in the energy industry for more than 25 years, most recently working in the emerging worldwide renewable energy sector.

While at Shell International, he was responsible for business activities in energy management, solar and heat pump operations. He also established electricity generation businesses and was the founding MD of Shell Power Limited. Peter then moved to Nuclear Electric as head of sales and marketing, before becoming MD of Midlands Gas.

More recently, Peter has advised renewable project developers, energy users and financiers in arrangements to produce and acquire renewable fuels and electricity. He has assisted major companies in establishing and implementing 'green' strategies. Peter joined Utilyx in 2007.

For further details see: www.utilyx.com

25 Renewable energy solutions

Companies have been racing headlong to embrace renewable projects that reduce their environmental impact – but have they chosen wisely? Chris Bowden, Chief Executive of energy and climate risk consultants Utilyx, reports.

Renewable, or green, energy solutions have become very fashionable in the business community over the last couple of years. As climate change issues have risen to the top of corporate agendas the desire to be seen to be Green has now become a priority – but, in their rush to embrace renewable energy solutions, many CEOs have failed to understand the true complexity involved with implementing one.

But, renewable solutions aren't, however, as straightforward as they first appear. With 'buzz' words like carbon neutrality, offsetting and green energy filling boardrooms around the world the danger is that in their rush to announce new renewable energy projects, many solutions will fail to deliver on their promise – and add little to combating climate change or to the business. We have already seen much publicised, renewable projects criticised by some media outlets for failing to deliver on their initial promise. Worse, some have had to be rethought because they have either been unsustainable or have not been financially or operationally viable on a day-to-day basis.

Business benefit v environmental impact

Implementing a renewable energy solution can be as simple as a commitment to buy green energy from one of the increasing number of suppliers, or as complex as designing and building a generation facility powered by renewable, 'clean' fuel. It can also include adopting new procurement, energy trading and risk management policies (to include climate change in to existing energy price and consumption risk calculations). The challenge is determining which solution(s) will deliver maximum benefit for

Sustainable renewables

While sustainable energy is a must-have for many global businesses, it is not a quick or easy solution. The creation and day-to-day management of these projects needs careful research and planning in order to select the best possible solution that benefits the business as well as the environment. Building a sustainable energy solution requires both time and money, and be a part of a sustained climate change policy rolled out and evolved over many years – in many cases up to 30 years – rather than a short-term, ill-considered PR stunt.

Chris Bowden is CEO of Utilyx. He co-founded the company in 2000.

He has 20 years' experience in the commodity markets and started his career in the treasury department at N.M.Rothschild & Sons Ltd, which gave him an in-depth knowledge of risk management and finance. His roles included being manager of debt markets and derivatives trading.

Chris moved to Merrill Lynch International, where he was vice president, senior marketer responsible for marketing risk management products to natural resource-based companies in Europe, Africa and the Middle East. He advised several large utility companies on the structure of power selling agreements and energy risk management strategies.

Following Merrill Lynch, Chris took on the role of head derivatives trader at Scandic Energy, one of the world's first electricity trading companies. He was responsible for shaping the company's trading activities and was party to the world's first exchange-traded electricity option.

Chris is regularly invited to speak on TV and radio. He has contributed material for national broadsheet newspapers, radio and TV broadcasters and key industry publications. Chris is FSA accredited.

For further details see: www.utilyx.com

26 Planning for renewables

The use of renewables is set to increase dramatically.
Sarah Youren at Field Fisher Waterhouse looks at how
to get projects up and running.

The Government introduced the Renewables Obligation in 2002 which forced electricity suppliers to source an increasing percentage of their energy from renewable sources. The Government has now tabled proposals in the Energy White Paper to reform the Renewables Obligation system to form different bands to recognise that some renewable technologies are more advanced than others. It should reflect the practical constraints faced by the most mature technologies such as onshore wind, to give less support to cheaper technologies such as co-firing and to give much more support to the next generation of technologies such as offshore wind, wave and tidal.

Planning policy statement 22 set out the Government's aims to achieve 10% of UK energy generation from renewable sources by 2010 rising to 20% by 2020.

The Climate Change bill will take this a step further by introducing a legally binding target of reducing the UKs carbon emissions by 60% by 2050 compared to 1990 levels. An increase in renewable energy generation will be required to achieve this.

The EU is also stepping up the pressure by pledging last year to produce 20% of Europe's energy from renewable sources within 12 years. Europe is demanding that 15% of all the energy used in Britain for electricity, transport and heating comes from renewables. Britain is already committed to ensuring that 10% of the energy used for transport is biofuel (produced from crops rather than from oil) so further opportunities for green transport fuel are limited. It will also be difficult to use more green energy for heating as most UK homes have gas central heating boilers which are difficult to convert. This means the energy sector must mop up the rest of the target. According to the Government an astonishing 40% of the UK's electricity will have to be generated by renewable sources by 2020, compared with just 5% now. Most of that is expected to come from wind power. The UK already has around 2,000 wind turbines but the British Wind Energy Association estimate that another 5,000 will be needed on land and thousands more at sea to meet these targets.

The EU also wants to expand the carbon emissions trading scheme in which companies have to buy permits if they emit carbon dioxide. From 2013 the scheme will cover more industrial sectors while power companies will have to buy their permits at auction for the first time, rather than be handed them for free. For industries not covered by the scheme (such as transport and housing) the EU plans to set new national emissions targets. Before the EU's proposals come into force they will have to be endorsed by MEPs and member states. The final package may not come into force until the end of 2009. Any countries that fail to meet their targets will be fined.

Funding support from the Government

The Government is increasing support for energy innovation ranging from the research and development programmes supported by the Research Councils and the Technology Strategy Board to BERR's activities in support of demonstration and replication of renewable technologies. In 2008 BERR will be launching the new Energy Technologies Institute with a minimum budget of around £600 million over the next decade for research and development into low carbon energy drawing on private as well as public funding.

Support from the planning system

The Government believes the current planning system takes too long and is too unpredictable and complex to bring important infrastructure projects forward. Today there are 56 wind farm projects capable collectively of generating 4GW of energy that have been stuck in the planning system for over two years. If all of these projects had been approved and constructed we would now be 25% closer towards our 2010 target of production of 10% of the UK's energy from renewable sources. BERR's research has found that by 2006/7 nearly 50% of all planning applications for wind farms determined by local planning authorities were refused.

At present the planning system can be subject to delays for a variety of reasons. Information provided by developers may be incomplete. Regulators, whether in central or local government, may take too long to reach decisions, sometimes because they are waiting on critical inputs from the Government's statutory advisors on matters such as environmental impacts. Public inquiries can take a long time and there may be a wait for the report and decision afterwards. If the consent decision is judicially reviewed this adds another delay. Added to this is time at the pre-application stage and the construction period. In a worst case scenario there can be 7-10 years between a company taking an internal decision to invest and delivery of energy to the grid.

Through the Planning Bill the Government is creating an Infrastructure Planning Commission which will operate within National Policy Statements to bring greater transparency to the planning system, take ministers out of individual decisions and create a strong democratic framework for Parliament, public and civil society to engage.

In an effort to speed up the grant of planning permission for wind energy development in the UK the Government has issued a set of generic planning conditions which are considered to be relevant to wind farm development throughout the UK, and would serve as a starting point when considering the grant of planning permission.[1]

Should renewable energy be generated onsite or offsite?

Around 140 Council's are believed to have adopted renewable energy quotas following Merton Borough Council's pioneering example in 2003. Most require 10% of a new development's energy to come from onsite renewables (such as wind turbines or photovoltaic panels) although some, such

---

1. Onshore Wind Energy Planning Conditions Guidance Note October 2007

as Brighton, Oxford and the Greater London Authority are seeking 20%. For new developments requiring high levels of energy use, such as data centres, this means generating significant levels of renewable energy on site.

On 13 December 2007 the Government published a long awaited planning policy statement on climate change which says that quotas must be flexible and should only be used where it is viable. This is in response to lobbying from bodies such as the British Property Federation, who argue that blanket quotas are often unworkable in individual locations. Critics also argue that this blanket policy removed the scope for considering wider local low carbon opportunities. The planning policy statement is out to consultation until 8 March 2008.

In the meantime a private members bill called the Planning and Energy Bill had its first reading in the House of Commons in December 2007 and its second reading on 25 January 2008. It would formally give local authorities the power to include quotas for the amount of onsite renewable energy to be used in new developments within their development plans. This would prevent developers from using connections to off-site wind farms and other sources of renewable energy to meet the quotas. The Bill would also give the Councils the power to demand standards of energy efficiency that exceed current building regulations. There is a good prospect of this or something similar becoming legislation.

Microgeneration

According to the British Wind Energy Association the UK has the best wind resources in Europe and has the chance to become a world leader in small wind energy technologies. The DTI estimates that by 2050 up to 30-40% of the UK's electricity generation could be produced by small and micro-generation technologies including 6% from small wind energy generation. Small wind energy installations require planning permission and local consultation with relevant stakeholders such as neighbours. Deciding factors include environmental considerations, access to the site, noise and visual effects. National planning policy statement 22 supports the development of small scale wind energy subject to appropriate environmental safeguards.

Funding

There are several grant schemes which offer funding for small scale renewables, particularly for the domestic and community sector but also for businesses. The Low Carbon Buildings Programme (LCBP) started in April 2006 is managed by the Energy Saving Trust, and offers grants for domestic and community and larger microgeneration installations. In November 2005 the Energy Minister announced £30 million of funding over three years for the LCBP and in March 2006 a further £50 million was allocated to the programme.

There are two streams of funding. Stream 1 is a maximum of £1,000 per kW installed for householders and small businesses up to a total of £5,000 subject to an overall 30% limit of the installed cost. For community applications grants are up to 50% of the capital and installation costs of the microgeneration technologies installed to a maximum of £50,000.

Stream 2 is for large projects from not for profit community organisations, businesses, building developers, energy services companies and the public sector to install microgeneration on large scale building projects. Up to £100,000 per project is available on large retrofit projects. Up to £1 million is available per project for major refurbishment and new build projects.

Support from the planning system

PPS1 states that Regional Spatial Strategies should ensure that opportunities for renewable and low carbon sources of energy supply and supporting infrastructure, including decentralised energy supply systems, are maximised. Regional Spatial Strategies should set regional targets for renewable energy generation in line with PPS22. At a local level, when developing their core strategy and supporting local development documents, planning authorities should provide a framework that promotes and encourages renewable and low carbon energy generation. In particular they should not require applicants for energy development to demonstrate either the overall need for renewable energy and its distribution nor question the energy justification for why a proposal for such a development must be sited in a particular location.

Removing barriers to microgeneration

The Energy White Paper announced new arrangements to simplify the current regulatory system. All six major energy suppliers have committed to publishing clear and transparent tariffs for exported electricity so that households and businesses that generate their energy and export some to the grid can be clear about the financial benefit of doing so. Legislation in the Finance Bill 2007 will ensure that where private householders install microgeneration technology in their home for the purpose of generating power for their personal use, any payments they receive from the sale of surplus power or Renewable Obligations Certificates to an energy company will not be subject to income tax.

BERR have funded the development of an industry led scheme to certify installers and manufacturers of microgeneration equipment. BERR have also established a new Distributed Energy Unit to monitor the development of these technologies and identify and remove any further barriers to distributed energy.

Leading the way

Nicholas Stern estimated that the low carbon energy product market could be worth over $500 billion per year by 2050.

Ormiston Wire in Middlesex was one of the first industrial organisations to install a small 2.5kW wind turbine to reduce power consumption and save money. Many organisations have since followed, for example, Sainsburys which powers its store at Greenwich from on-site wind turbines in the car park.

Sarah is a partner in the Planning and Environment team at Field Fisher Waterhouse. She advises on all aspects of planning and environmental law from inception to construction of a project. Her clients include private developers, funders, local authorities and Government organisations.

The Planning and Environment team advise on all aspects of planning and environmental law. We have a particular interest in sustainable development and help clients obtain planning permission, evaluate Environmental Impact Assessments, negotiate planning and infrastructure agreements and acquire sites through compulsory purchase. On the environmental side we offer skilled and commercial advice on issues such as flooding, contaminated land, waste, water pollution and recycling. We have considerable experience in the energy field and with flood related development.

Further details: www.ffw.com

Part 6

Product lifecycles

27 Design for climate

Beatrice Otto looks at the scope for creating new innovations that can open up new markets or revolutionise them.

You're reading this book which is on managing climate risk, so you probably consider that climate change is potentially a risk to your company. By the end of reading this chapter, you may also be thinking about the opportunities it could bring to your business.

How do you 'design for climate'? Depending on the nature of your business, you might prioritise according to the energy use and climate impacts of your operations – procurement, production, distribution, disposal, property – or of your products and services. We'll move through that spectrum in a moment but first, a quick flip of a two-sided coin to limber you up.

Risk reduction

> *"Climate change is now seen as one of the defining challenges of the 21st century... the way in which climate change is dealt with at the global level will be a leading indicator of the world's capacity to manage globalization in an equitable and sustainable way."*
>
> World Economic Forum, Global Risks 2007

Where are you on the risk scale? Are you (or could you be) exposed to:

- *production time-outs* due to black-outs in regions where energy supply can't keep pace with demand

- *regulatory thumb-screws* as emission reduction targets begin to bite, percolating down from lofty goals to legal constraints

- *client questions* as they start factoring suppliers' greenhouse gas emissions into their own carbon foot-printing; both corporate and public procurement are likely to become more stringent in scrutinising suppliers' climate impacts

- *consumer questions* as growing concern about climate change, or more prosaically, about climbing energy costs, make them look at energy labels

- *reduced competitiveness* as those same rising energy costs erode your profitability

- *reputational damage* from not cutting the mustard in responding to climate change, compared to your competitors.

Opportunity knocks

> *"We are going to solve tough customer and global problems and make money doing it."*
>
> Jeff Immelt, CEO, General Electric

GE stole a march on some of their competitors with their Ecoimagination campaign, providing a shot in the arm to their brand. Putting their money where their mouth is, they aim to double their profits from clean technology business to $US 20 billion by 2010.

Energetically addressing climate risk can translate into some enticing opportunities for running a leaner, meaner machine, increasing market share, creating new products or services, such as:

- *using less energy* in your operations will reduce costs, so far so simple

- *(re)designing products or services* to save energy and slash the emissions of customers could expand your markets, as could products or services which address the adaptation side of climate change

- *strengthening your brand* even if your customer doesn't directly gain from your new and improved climate-friendly behaviour

- *keeping a step ahead of the regulator* – compliance is becoming the basic entry ticket, and thinking beyond compliance could yield greater returns than staying just the right side of the law.

Getting your house in order

Before you plunge in, do a big picture brain-storming about where your greatest risks and opportunities lie. You could become bogged down in the minutiae of wringing ever greater savings in your own energy use while missing the cornucopia that an innovative design could yield in customers' energy use. You can redesign a mobile phone to use less of this or that, or to be easily recycled, but think laterally too. How can a mobile phone reduce transport emissions by allowing the user to travel less or avoid traffic jams?

Pick the low hanging fruit

Energy efficiency has been described as the fifth energy source, and one that is pretty universally available, under-exploited and relatively cheap. The International Energy Agency has calculated that every dollar invested in energy efficiency saves more than two dollars' investment in energy supply. They also reckon that about 80% of avoided carbon emissions can come from energy efficiency. Start here, and only when you have made your energy use more svelte, move to parking that beautiful wind turbine on the roof.

Brain gain

You've picked the low hanging fruit, now pick employees' brains on the next steps. Companies that have instituted idea-gathering mechanisms have often been astonished at the wealth of innovation that has poured in. Some thought that once the low hanging fruit had been plucked, the flow would slow but, in fact, the converse proved true. Make it a competition if you want, but tap that intangible asset one way or another.

Way back in 1998, before climate change was a daily headline, BP decided to reduce its carbon emissions by 10% by 2010 (against a 1990 baseline). They garnered ideas in-house, hundreds of them, and hit their target nine years ahead of schedule. But the return on investment is what should excite the reader: it cost them US$ 20 million but they found it added US$ 650 million of value to the firm.

While you're in brain-storming mode, attack your products and services. Any mitigation of climate change you can engender within the company can be dwarfed by the improvements you can make to your customers' carbon foot-prints, such as by:

- *(Re)designing products* to cut emissions and save energy, or by generating or tapping into renewable sources of energy.

- *Shifting to a more performance based business model.* Moving from a product-based to a performance-based model can enhance profits. For example, some paint producers have shifted from selling pots (or vats) of paint to selling paint services. Since they're being paid to paint and not for paint, they have an incentive to come up with ways to reduce the amount of paint needed per Product X, using their superior knowledge of paint. Make the end point your starting point – not your product, but the results your customer seeks. They don't buy a radiator because they want a radiator, but because they want heat.

- *Looping the loop.* It might make sense to keep a product or its components in use for longer (assuming no technological over-taking renders today's product clunkily obsolete), possibly offering leasing deals with maintenance contracts that allow you to recoup and reprocess materials or parts.

- *Adaptation innovation.* There are opportunities not only in mitigating climate change but in adapting to it. For example, if climate change increases water scarcity on the one hand and flooding on the other, then the market for products and services that improve water management or flood control could flourish alongside those focusing directly on energy efficiency, renewable energy or carbon-cuts.

And don't assume that this only works for multinational giants. A report by Shell Springboard/Vivid Economics, demonstrates the importance of small and medium-sized enterprises (SMEs) in tackling climate change. It identifies some key markets, including:

- *Regulatory requirements for buildings* – buildings are responsible for about 40% of global emissions. Moving beyond the building itself are the opportunities for reducing the heat island effect – the higher ambient temperatures of built-up areas – thereby reducing the cooling load on buildings and helping to counteract urban-based temperature increases resulting from climate change. Examples might be heat-reflective surfaces, and better use of moisture and shading to generate cooling.

- *Renewable energy* – the Cleantech Group says that investments in this area passed the US$ 5 billion mark last year, an increase of 44% on the previous year.

The same report points out that SMEs can access all areas of the markets emerging for energy efficiency, renewable energy and other responses to the climate challenge.

Even large scale infrastructure projects often use SMEs as subcontractors, and use the innovations created by SMEs. SMEs are ideally placed to create new innovations that open up new markets or revolutionise them.

Go forth and prosper.

References

- Shell Springboard/Vivid Economics, *The business opportunities for SMEs* in tackling the causes of climate change, October 2006 (www.shellspringboard.org). In addition to a concise scan of the opportunity landscape for SMEs, this report also gives a number of examples of SMEs which are already tapping in.

- CBI Climate Change Task Force, *Climate change: Everyone's business*, November 2007 (www.cbi.org.uk). A crystal clear, well designed summary of why climate change matters to business.

- World Business Council for Sustainable Development, *Energy Efficiency in Buildings: Business realities and opportunities*, August 2007 (www.wbcsd.org).

- American Solar Energy Society, *Renewable Energy and Energy Efficiency: Economic Drivers for the 21st Century*, 2007 (www.ases.org). Although focusing on the US market, this is nevertheless a good overview of emerging opportunities.

- Paul Hawken, Amory Lovins, L. Hunter Lovins, *Natural Capitalism: Creating the next industrial revolution*, Back Bay Books, 2000. This should be on your short-list of books worth reading. It gives the big picture but dozens of clear examples.

- Joseph Romm, *Cool Companies: How the best businesses boost profits and productivity by cutting greenhouse gas emissions*, Island Press, 2006. One of the best books for laying out why and how to do what the title says. It shows some astonishing gains for companies, and should help you formulate your own priorities.

- Bjorn Lomborg, *Cool It: The skeptical environmentalist's guide to global warming*, Marshall Cavendish, 2007. This level-headed, readable guide gives more context to what is going on behind the hype and the headlines, and aims to set some priorities.

Beatrice Otto (ottobeatrice@hotmail.com) authors the Design Council's expert article on Sustainable Design (http://www.designcouncil.org.uk/en/About-Design/Business-Essentials/Sustainability/), which gives a short, sharp overview of the issues and opportunities in sustainable design, and directions to some of the best books, journals, tools and web-sites, while sparing you information overload.

28 Funding for clean technologies

In the last two years, venture capitalists have left the margins and have started to treat low-carbon technologies as a mainstream area of investment activity, reports Alice Chapple, Director of Sustainable Financial Markets at Forum for the Future.

Faced with climate change and resource depletion, it is clear that a massive shift is needed to develop a low-carbon global economy and to improve resource efficiency. This can only happen with significant investment. This chapter considers the sources of investment for clean technologies or 'clean-tech', particularly for small and medium-sized enterprises.

The landscape for funding for clean technologies has evolved considerably over the last two to three years.

The first generation of clean technology companies was largely focused on the environmental protection space. Many did not have business plans, technologies were embryonic and markets were completely dependent on regulation. The entrepreneurs in the sector were often motivated by the environmental benefit of their product or service, rather than by the potential for high financial returns. For venture capitalists, the proposition was not an attractive one.

The transformation over the last two years has been remarkable. Concerns about energy security, increasing oil prices and climate change have created impetus for investment in the clean energy sector. The momentum has been supported by the scientific view of the timeframe over which transformation to a low-carbon economy has to take place to avoid dangerous climate change. This indicates that urgent action is needed now, rather than a deferral of investment until the technological solutions mature. Government policy is beginning to move to support investment in this transition and, importantly, the market understands the need for regulation. Beyond the clean energy sector, increasing pressure on natural resources resulting from increasing populations and growing affluence is also a trend that some investors recognise as a key driver of value in the future, influencing the way in which businesses procure, manufacture, sell and dispose of their products.

The rapid growth of interest in these types of business has resulted in a new sector classification known to investors as cleantech. The Cleantech Venture Network tracks a number of subsectors within this investment space, and there are several different types of business, as shown in the table below.

Cleantech subsectors
• Agriculture & Nutrition
• Air Quality
• Enabling technologies
• Energy related
• Environmental IT
• Manufacturing/Industrial
• Materials & Nanotechnology
• Materials recovery & recycling
• Transportation & logistics
• Water purification & management

Cleantech Business Type	Key features	Examples
Cleantech SMEs	Smaller companies that apply already developed technologies or provide other ancillary services. They usually do not have very fast or high growth potential but are important for environmental and employment reasons.	Wind & solar household installation Niche green products (e.g. construction)
Technology start-ups	Young companies commercializing technologies into products and entering markets with good growth potential.	Ceres Power Nanosolar
Pure Play cleantech	Cleantech firms that have developed into significant independent corporations, usually publicly listed and making the majority of revenue from cleantech as core business.	Vestas Wind Suzlon Energy SolarTech
Traditional environmental goods & services	Water utilities and waste management companies, including large private or public firms and a wide range of smaller waste management companies, environmental consultancies etc.	Severn Trent SITA Veolia
Subsidiaries	Business units within major corporations involved in cleantech, which form a small part of the overall business.	General Electric Mitsubishi Sharp

Table 1: Cleantech subsectors and business types

The changing attitude of venture capital investors to clean technologies is reflected in the numbers. Worldwide venture capital investment of $2.5 billion into the cleantech space in 2005 was followed by investment of $3.6 billion in 2006 and $5.18 billion in 2007.[1] The bulk of this cleantech investment ($2.75bn in 2007 or 53%) was in low-carbon technologies. However, water, waste management and resource efficiency investments also featured strongly.

1 Source: Cleantech Group LLC

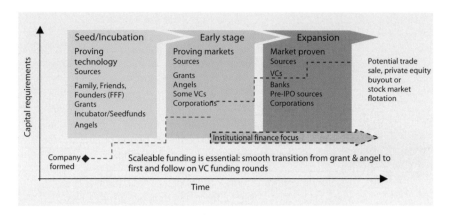

Figure1: Funding sources at different stages of investment

Fundamental market drivers have been accompanied by a growing sophistication of companies in the cleantech space. The basic requirements from a potential funder of early-stage cleantech are no different from in other sectors. So an early-stage cleantech deal needs to show an acceptable risk-reward profile, a scaleable business model with a defined route to market, a clear mechanism for the venture capital firm to exit its investment after 3-6 years, and strong management skills.

Risk-reward profile	VCs assume very high levels of risk but need to ensure that potential returns on investment can justify that exposure. Typically, minimum rates of return will exceed 20-25%.
Growth, scalability and market prospects	Firms need a clearly defined route to market, evidence of verifiable market potential with high growth prospects and a scaleable business model. Markets driven by environmental regulation are unreliable due to high public policy risk and VCs prefer proven demand. Strong Intellectual Property Rights (IPR) are also essential for innovative technology based ventures.

Exit routes & time horizon	VCs need to see a clear mechanism for 'exiting' their investments and realising returns. Exits normally happen through flotation on the stockmarket (IPO), or sale of the stake to another investor, company management or through a merger. Most VCs prefer to operate within a 3-6 year timeframe and are constrained by capital structures – normally a 10 year closed end fund structure for most firms – which means that investments and returns must be realised within this period. The long gestation period on many clean technologies makes investment challenging.
Management capability	Strong entrepreneurial skills and excellent management capability are essential to develop technology potential into viable businesses. VCs prefer experienced entrepreneurs and management teams. This is often an issue in the cleantech sector, where much is new.
Deal size	To manage risk and assess investments, VCs undertake rigorous due diligence. Consequently, they have very high fixed transaction costs requiring deals of a sufficient size to warrant management attention. Most VCs typically start investing in the £1-2million range.

Table 2: Generic requirements of venture capital funds

Source: Clean Capital, Forum for the Future, January 2007

Governments have developed specific schemes to offer both equity and debt support to SMEs, in an attempt to address some issues identified in the supply of finance for cleantech. In the UK in 2006, the public sector participated in over 45% of all cleantech deals, whereas the average for Europe as a whole was just 14.7%.[2] In the US, schemes such as the Small Business Innovation Research Programme, and the involvement of experienced and successful entrepreneurs in the cleantech space, are cited as a key reason for the relatively high levels of US investment in this sector.

2 Source: Cleantech Goes Mainstream, Library House, April 2007

Issue	Explanation	Solutions to explore in the UK context
Lack of investment readiness	Inadequate business plans, including cash flows, route to market, range of management experience.	Investment readiness programmes (eg E-Synergy in partnership with the Carbon Trust)
Difficulties accessing equity finance (under £250,000) at seed stage	Very small deal size is below VC threshold.	Regional Venture Capital Funds (RVCFs) – capitalised by public money but managed by professional VC managers, they have a small cleantech portfolio

Cleantech angel networks (AngelBourse, Cleantech Venture Network) |
| "Valley of death" between £250,000 and £2m | Some research has identified an equity gap between £250,000 and £2m. | Enterprise Capital Funds (ECFs) – commercially run and investing a mix of public and private money into small firms with capacity for high growth

Enterprise Investment Scheme – business angels are offered a tax incentive for investing in start-ups |
| Time spent chasing follow-on funding | Executives spend considerable time chasing small sums every 6-10 months, detracting attention from core business. | Follow-on funding from govt schemes

Early contact with venture capital funds active in this space |
| Finance for pre-commercial pilots and demonstrators | Technology demonstrators are essential to many cleantech firms attracting customers but are very high risk for financiers and may also require significant capital. | Small Firms Loan Guarantee – allows small companies to access conventional banking loans with Government acting as a guarantor.

Public procurement – eg in the UK, the Forward Commitment Initiative |

Table 3: Issues in the supply of finance to early-stage cleantech companies

The different types and levels of support provided by different governments plays a part in determining not only the volume but also the direction of cleantech investment. The UK's funding is focused more on early-stage support whilst in Germany, for example, the support has been largely in the form of feed-in tariffs for renewable energy. This has played a part in an interesting variation in the composition of cleantech investment in the two countries, as illustrated below.

UK

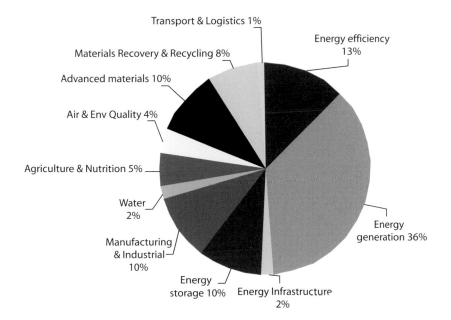

Source: Cleantech Venture Network

Germany

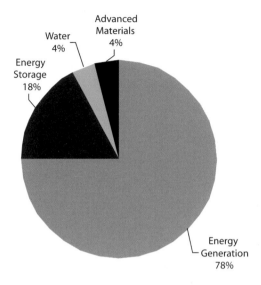

Water 4%

Advanced Materials 4%

Energy Storage 18%

Energy Generation 78%

Source: Cleantech Venture Network

There is limited concentration in terms of the key venture capital investors. In Europe in 2006, there were 102 institutional cleantech deals but no one venture capital firm participated in more than 5 of them.[3] The large mainstream venture capital companies, such as 3i and Quester Partners in Europe,[4] have made the greatest number of investments. However, specialist cleantech venture capital firms are beginning to emerge and some observers consider that this will be a critical step in developing the detailed analysis that is required to continue the expansion of investment in the cleantech space at the pace that is required.

According to a report by UNEP, SEFI and New Energy Finance,[5] investment in clean energy across all stages, including R&D, seed finance, venture capital, asset finance and mergers and acquisitions exceeded $100 billion

---

3 Source: Cleantech Goes Mainstream, Library House, April 2007

4 In the US, the largest VC funders of cleantech are also mainstream funds – Kleiner Perkins Caulfield & Byers, Khosla Ventures and Draper Fisher Jurvetson.

5 UNEP, SEFI and New Energy Finance, Global Trends in Sustainable Energy Investment 2007

in 2006. The report comments: "The finance community has been investing at levels that imply that expected disruptive change is now inevitable in the energy sector." Climate change and resource depletion will also require radical transformation in other 'cleantech' areas – transportation, water, waste, packaging, advanced materials, agriculture. Investors' appetite for this sector is increasing. The fundamental drivers are in place, supported by government schemes. Investment in cleantech will continue to grow at all stages of the investment cycle. With the right ideas, project plans and management skills, SMEs will play a crucial role in developing this vital sector.

Alice Chapple is Director of Sustainable Financial Markets at Forum for the Future, the sustainable development charity. Forum works in partnership with leading organisations in business and the public sector. Its vision is of business and communities thriving in a future that is environmentally sustainable and socially just. The Sustainable Financial Markets programme investigates the current and future role of the financial system in allocating capital to sustainable activities. Alice can be contacted on a.chapple@forumforthefuture.org.uk

29 Carbon footprinting

Carbon footprinting is the technique of choice for substantiating claims about the impact of a product or an organisation on the climate. Charles Allison at ERM examines how it works.

This chapter provides an introduction to carbon footprinting for business under the following headings:

- What is a carbon footprint?
- Why use carbon footprinting?
- Methodologies and definitions
- Developing the carbon footprint of an organisation
- Developing the carbon footprint of a product
- Communicating and using carbon footprints

What is a carbon footprint?

Simply stated, a carbon footprint is the total emissions of carbon dioxide and its equivalents of other greenhouse gases, for a defined system or activity.

Everything has a carbon footprint: you and I as individuals, the businesses and organisations in which we work and the towns and countries in which we live. Projects (for example, the building or modification of an office block, a road or railway line, or an industrial process) also have a carbon footprint.

For the purposes of the carbon footprint each individual, for example, becomes the 'system' and we draw a 'system boundary' around all activities undertaken, from travelling to work to using energy to keeping warm. For companies, particularly those with lengthy supply chains, the challenge can be more complex. A food retailer, for example, may look at both its direct footprint caused by stores, deliveries etc., but may also want to consider the indirect impacts caused by suppliers and by customers. The challenge for businesses is to present a clear and accurate picture of what is being calculated.

Why use carbon footprinting?

Businesses use carbon footprinting to calculate the carbon impact of their operations (including goods and services) and as a basis for a future carbon reduction strategy. Developing an accurate picture of your company's carbon footprint will also support effective carbon disclosure which is becoming a requirement for all types of business. A company which has an accurate picture of its carbon footprint is not only helping to ensure future compliance but can also enhance its reputation for effective environmental management and transparency.

Carbon footprinting and carbon reduction is also another way of engaging customers and influencing their buying behaviour. A growing number of consumers are concerned about climate change and are looking for products and services – for example, a low energy loaf or carbon neutral train journey – which address this issue. Food that has been sourced locally or produced using less energy may well become a more attractive option.

Consumers are becoming more conscious of their own carbon footprint which in turn is having an influence on their buying habits. The graph below shows a breakdown of the carbon footprint of 'Mr or Mrs Average' in the UK, amounting to somewhere between 10 and 12 tonnes of carbon dioxide equivalents (CO_2e) per year(see Figure 1).

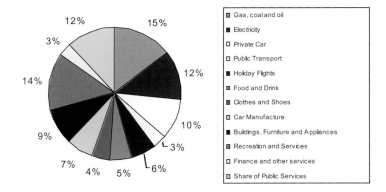

Figure 1: Average CO$_2$ emission per person in UK

Consumers can typically reduce their impact, either by reducing the carbon footprint of the products and services that they buy (which drives demand for carbon footprint data) or by paying to invest in carbon reduction projects to 'offset' the resulting emissions. Recent announcements around a possible approach to carbon labelling of consumer goods, applying a standard that will be developed by Defra, the Carbon Trust and BSI British Standards, paint a picture of likely developments in this area.

As noted above, companies are under pressure to measure and disclose their corporate carbon footprints from investors and other stakeholders. They want to see greater and better disclosure by large companies on their climate-related risks and opportunities. Investor coalitions such as the Carbon Disclosure Project and related investment indices such as the Dow Jones Sustainability Index, UK BITC CR Index, and FTSE4Good Index, all require companies to disclose their carbon footprint and report on their carbon reduction targets and performance annually. Indeed, some investors (particularly the major investment banks) are coming under attack from pressure groups who are asking them to disclose the carbon emissions resulting from the companies in which they invest.

With regard to offsetting, there have been a number of scare stories (some fair and others not) relating to the nature of the offset and its actual contribution to carbon reduction. More product and service providers are marketing 'carbon neutral' offerings and the government is looking to regulate the sector through development of a code of practice. The Advertising Standards Authority, which already has a remit to deal with phoney or misleading 'green claims', has never been so busy. The onus is on companies to calculate their footprints accurately, communicate them transparently and fully support their claims of environmental improvement.

A third category of demand for carbon footprinting comes from stakeholders of projects. For example, a planning or development authority may want to know the carbon footprint of a proposal to build a new airport terminal or road link. The UK Government's Code for Sustainable Homes and plans to make all new homes 'zero carbon' by 2016, will require developers to, in effect, demonstrate the carbon footprint of individual buildings. Emerging best practice is already moving beyond this, to consider the carbon footprint of whole developments, considering not just the impacts of the buildings themselves, but also the impacts of related travel and the need for low-carbon transport options.

Finally, in the carbon markets, there is a need to calculate the carbon impact of projects (often termed a 'greenhouse gas inventory'). Now that carbon is a tradable commodity, projects that result in a reduction in emissions, typically in the developing world, can generate 'credits' which have a value of somewhere between £5 – £15 per tonne of CO_2. These projects can range from improving energy efficiency in industrial processes, to reducing emissions of the greenhouse gas methane from landfill sites. To deliver these credits, there is a need to calculate, and verify, the reduction in emissions that result from the project, compared to the pre-project 'baseline'.

In a world where, increasingly, carbon will have a significant monetary value, business faces the challenge of measuring its impact in order to manage and ultimately reduce emissions. Carbon footprinting has rapidly emerged as the methodology that organisations use to calculate performance, identify priorities and measure progress over time. Those who get it right can be confident of sending out a positive message to customers, investors and other stakeholders.

Methodologies and definitions

There are already plenty of definitional issues when it comes to calculating carbon footprints. Where do you draw the 'system boundary' or 'scope' of the footprint? What 'greenhouse gases' do you include? Do you quote the footprint in terms of Carbon (C), carbon dioxide (CO_2), or carbon dioxide equivalents (CO_2e)?

Here is a checklist of some carbon footprint basics:

- The standard reporting unit is tonnes of CO_2 equivalent (tCO_2e).

- There are six main greenhouse gases (the 'Kyoto basket of six') for carbon footprint calculations (see Table 1 below). Some of these have a 'global warming potential' that is many times greater than that of CO_2 (for example, 1 tonne of methane has the same global warming impact as 23 tonnes of CO_2).

- The 'boundary' or scope of a carbon footprint can be drawn narrowly for a specific activity (typically this will be referred to as a direct footprint since it considers only the emissions that arise directly from that activity) or broadly (including emissions indirectly associated with the activity).

- Whatever the boundary, the approach to calculating a carbon footprint follows the same approach as this example for grid electricity:

  Activity data x emissions factor x global warming potential = GHG emissions

  $(10,000 \text{ kWh}) \times (0.43 \text{kg } CO_2/\text{kWh}) \times (1) = 4.30 \text{ tonnes} CO_2e$

- There are several reputable sources for emission factors, including international bodies such as the United Nations' Intergovernmental Panel on Climate Change, and national government departments such as the Department of the Environment, Food and Rural Affairs (Defra) in the UK.

Greenhouse Gas	Global Warming Potential	Key Industrial Sources
Carbon Dioxide (CO_2)	1	Combustion of fossil fuels; cement manufacture.
Methane (CH_4)	23	Oil & gas extraction and processing; mining; landfills; wastewater and sludge treatment.
Nitrous Oxide (N_2O)	296	Adipic acid and nitric acid production; wastewater treatment; combustion processes.
Hydrofluorocarbons (HFCs) and Hydrochlorofluorocarbons (HCFCs)	140 - 11,700	Refrigerant manufacture and use.
Perfluorocarbons (PFCs)	6,500 - 9,200	Refrigerant manufacture and use; Al and Mg smelting.
Sulphur Hexafluoride (SF_6)	23,900	Aluminium and magnesium smelting; high voltage electrical switching equipment.

Table 1: The Kyoto Basket of Six Major Greenhouse Gases

Developing the carbon footprint of an organisation

Step 1: Drawing the boundary

The first question for an organisation is where to draw the boundary. The Greenhouse Gas Accounting Protocol, drawn up by the World Business Council for Sustainable Development (WBCSD) and the World Resources Institute, is the main international source of guidance on organisational carbon footprinting. It defines procedures for determining emissions boundaries in terms of GHGs/sources and direct (known as 'Scope 1') and indirect ('Scope 2 and 3') emissions.

One of the most commonly used scopes for organisational reporting is the 'operational control boundary'. This states that organisations will calculate and take responsibility for those emissions that are under their operational control. This will include some emissions that occur outside of the organisation's own facilities (e.g. emissions from power stations) where those emissions result directly from the activities of the organisation (e.g. through consumption of electricity).

Whilst guidance on these matters does exist (eg WBCSD above, and at national level from government bodies such as Defra) there is considerable room for interpretation. In view of the increasing demand for transparency and accuracy, leading companies are tending to demonstrate graphically the boundaries of what they are calculating, reporting and taking responsibility for.

Figure 2 below shows an example boundary for a supermarket chain. Key boundary questions may arise in relation to assets where the supermarket has brand association but at best limited operational control (e.g. a branded food outlet at a petrol station, operated by the petrol station operator, or a distribution lorry which is painted in supermarket livery but is operated by a third party logistics company).

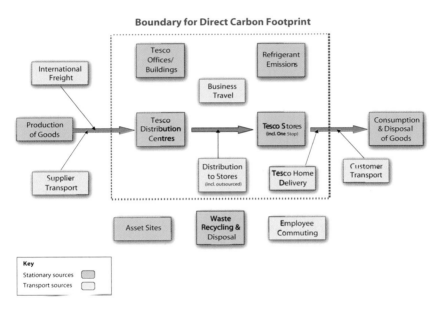

Figure 2: footprint boundaries

Step 2: Gather the data and apply emissions factors

Once the boundary and scope of the footprint has been agreed, it's time to gather appropriate activity data (e.g. fuel use, miles flown, refrigerant leakage) and application of the appropriate emissions factors and global warming potentials. Some emissions factors will change over time (e.g. the emissions factor for grid electricity at national level will change each year depending on the mix of energy sources – coal, gas, nuclear and renewables – in the national grid.

As always when working with organisational information, it is important to double check base data and units, and to sense check the results. It is likely, when an organisation calculates its footprint for the first time, that it will not have available a full set of all of the base data that is needed and will have to make estimates based on appropriate assumptions, or extrapolations of available data, may be needed. This should be acknowledged in the communication of the footprint, and appropriate data-gathering processes should be established so that, going forward, the footprint calculation is based on a robust and reliable set of base data.

Developing the carbon footprint of a product

Developing a product carbon footprint follows a similar approach to that of an organisation (i.e. activity data x emissions factor). The main difference is that a life-cycle approach is taken, which calculates robustly all of the potential GHG emissions associated with a product, process or service activity, including across its life-cycle:

- raw materials extraction
- processing
- manufacturing
- use
- disposal.

At each 'life cycle stage', natural resources are consumed and GHGs are released into the atmosphere, leading to a carbon footprint.

An extensive body of literature and technical best practice has been built in the area of Life Cycle Assessment (LCA). One aspect of this is the availability of 'Life Cycle Inventories' of validated data on the environmental impacts (including CO_2e emissions) from a wide range of typical activities. These can be applied when raw data is not available, to assist the development of product carbon footprints.

The boundary of a product carbon footprint will typically be drawn to cover all stages of its lifecycle. Alternatively, it could be drawn for all life cycle stages up to and including the retail shelf (i.e. excluding the impacts of consumption by the end user).

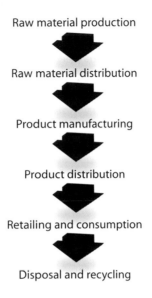

Raw material production

Raw material distribution

Product manufacturing

Product distribution

Retailing and consumption

Disposal and recycling

Figure 3: Product life cycle stages

A product carbon footprint will then be developed by calculating activity data and applying emissions factors for each relevant activity in each stage of the life cycle, as shown in Figure 4.

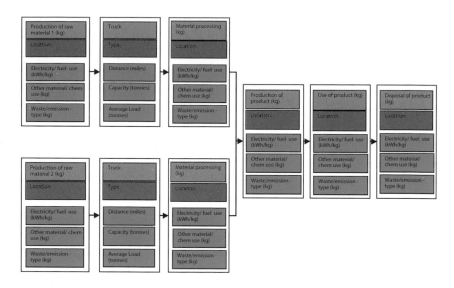

Figure 4: Product carbon footprinting method

This approach is most appropriate for analysis of a single product or product type. In other cases (e.g. where there is a need to assess the carbon footprint of whole categories of products or consumption activity (e.g. dairy products, shopping) other analytical approaches can be used. Input:output (I/O) analysis is a 'top-down' approach that includes all activities related to a product/service, takes the whole economy into account and is not limited by system boundaries. This makes it well-suited to estimation of carbon footprints from complex sectoral activities.

Communicating and using carbon footprints

Many organisations, particularly larger companies that are subject to scrutiny from stakeholders, or those that are making marketing claims (e.g. 'carbon neutral') based on carbon footprint information, will find value from some assurance/verification of their calculations by a credible third party. This will help them to maintain the confidence of their various stake-holders that the claims are robust and well-founded.

As well as being of use with external stakeholders, carbon footprint information can be very valuable within an organisation, highlighting opportunities for efficiency improvements and new ways of working:

Organisational footprint data can be cut by country of operation; by emission source (e.g. grid electricity, heating fuel, business travel etc.). This can support assessment of the carbon intensity of operations, typically expressed in terms of metrics such as tonnes CO_2e per unit of revenue, profit, production volume, area of floor space, etc (see Figure 5).

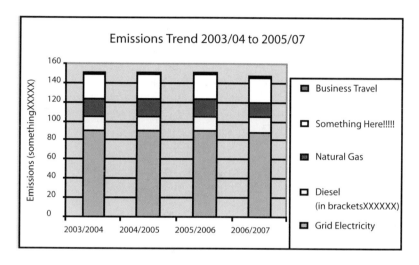

Figure 5: Example organisational carbon footprint – trend over time

Product footprint data can be analysed by lifecycle stage of the product, and by component/sub-component/ingredient (see Figure 6). This can be used to assess the impact of different product design and supply chain choices (see Figure 7) and also identify opportunities for product innovation.

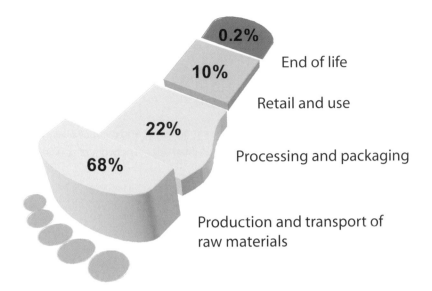

0.2%

End of life

10%

Retail and use

22%

Processing and packaging

68%

Production and transport of
raw materials

Figure 6: Product carbon footprint by lifecycle stage

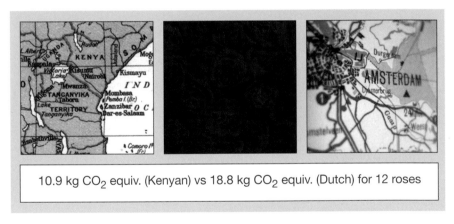

10.9 kg CO$_2$ equiv. (Kenyan) vs 18.8 kg CO$_2$ equiv. (Dutch) for 12 roses

Figure 7: Carbon footprint of alternative supply chains – Kenyan vs. Dutch roses

In summary, carbon footprinting can be applied at organisational, product and project level. It can be used in communicating environmental issues to an organisation's stakeholders, to identify and enable improvements in environmental performance by identifying opportunities for innovation and greater efficiencies.

For more information about carbon footprinting and ERM's services related to carbon, please contact Charles Allison at charles.allison@erm.com. ERM is a leading global environmental and sustainability consultancy. We are assisting a significant number of FTSE100, Fortune500 and government organisations to respond effectively to the challenges posed by climate change. Our suite of carbon management and climate change services is delivered to clients through an international network of specialists in all major world regions.

30 Waste management

Controls are becoming ever tighter on the disposal of waste, reports Rebecca Cushing at Field Fisher Waterhouse.

In its 2006 report '*Spotlight on Business*', the Environment Agency set out some startling facts regarding the nation's predilection for generating waste. The UK produces around 330 million tonnes of waste annually, a quarter of which is from households and business. The rest comes from construction and demolition, sewage, sludge, farm waste and spoils from mines and dredging of rivers[1]. England alone produces approximately 272 million tonnes of waste each year, 91% of which is non-household. More than one million tonnes of it consists of electrical equipment. About ten million tonnes of it consists of packaging waste[2]. In each case, most of this waste is disposed of in landfill sites.

However, whilst the total volume of waste landfilled in England and Wales decreased 1.5% between 2000 and 2005, at the same time landfill capacity dropped 10%. The industries regulated by the Environment Agency produced 42% more waste in 2006 than in 2000 although the proportion of waste recovered for further use in 2006 actually fell from 59% in 2005 to 51% in 2006. Whilst the amount of waste produced is growing, places in which to put it are running out.

Growing concern in the European Union about these waste streams and their environmental impact has led to the implementation of a number of 'Producer Responsibility' Directives which utilise the principle of 'the polluter pays'. These Regulations seek to ensure that the environmental impact of waste products is minimised by management through re-cycling and re-use. The European Union wishes to ensure that businesses are required to take financial responsibility for the environmental impact of products they place on the market, especially when those products become waste. The first of these Directives was the Packaging Waste Directive, which was implemented into domestic law in 1997, and subsequently amended. It has been

---

1   Source: Environment Agency website
2   Source: NetRegs website

followed by Producer Responsibility Directives on End of Life Vehicles, Waste Electronic and Electrical Equipment (WEEE) and there will be a forthcoming Directive on Batteries and Accumulators. All of these have been classified as priority waste streams due to growing concern over their impact on the environment. In addition, voluntary Producer Responsibility agreements have been established with certain business sectors, for example to increase the recycling of newspapers and direct mail.

The emphasis of waste legislation is to make business responsible for what it wants to dispose of and to set down rules controlling how that disposal takes place. Whilst consumers are not directly affected there is clearly a desire by the Environment Agency and other environmental regulators for end-users to deal with waste products responsibly as well.

General waste management

Over the years, regulation regarding waste minimisation and control has become more detailed and rigid. It is no longer just a question of disposing of unwanted material responsibly by taking it to the dump. Every business which produces, imports, transports, stores, treats or disposes of waste from business or industry has a duty to ensure that it is handled safely and in accordance with the law. This is known as the duty of care. This duty of care is unique in that it has no expiration; it continues until such time as a business has competently and correctly disposed of or recovered waste and can account for it. In addition, householders in England and Wales have a duty to ensure that household waste is collected by an appropriately authorised entity.

All commercial, industrial and household waste is classified as controlled waste and the duty of care applies to all controlled waste. Separate guidelines apply to controlled waste which is considered hazardous. The duty of care means that waste must be stored in a responsible manner and disposed of by authorised personnel. On a practical level this means keeping waste material confined and secure so that it does not pollute the environment, and ensuring that anyone who is paid to remove and dispose of the waste is correctly authorised to do so. The responsibility lies with the business to check the credentials of the company that is employed to take the waste away. It is incumbent upon business to check that anyone to whom waste is passed is authorised to take it; if such checks are not made and the waste is subsequently disposed of in an illegal manner, the business could be held responsible. Each waste carrier must have either an environmental permit if operating in England and Wales or a waste management licence if operating in Northern Ireland or Scotland, be registered to carry controlled waste (or have an exemption from registration), or come from a waste collection authority.

Responsibility for the waste does not end with its removal from site but only when it has been fully recovered or properly disposed of at an authorised or exempt treatment facility, even if the business has employed someone to do this on their behalf. Again, the onus is on the business to check that the final destination for the waste is correctly licensed.

As well as a need to check licenses there is an amount of paperwork to complete and retain by the business whose waste is being removed. A waste transfer note is required to accompany the waste being transported, providing a description of the quantity and type of waste that is being taken away in accordance with codes published by the Environment Agency. The notes must be signed by the waste carrier and the business prior to the waste leaving the business premises. Businesses and waste carriers must keep records of waste transferred or received for at least 2 years.

One further point to note is that the types of material that can legitimately be disposed of in landfill is becoming more limited. As of October 2007 it is illegal to put any liquid waste in landfill. Furthermore, all waste must now be 'treated' before being sent to landfill. This can be done by the business itself or by a later holder of the waste. Treating can mean anything from composting waste to collecting it according to its type in order to enable recycling. The idea is to encourage businesses to think about what happens to their waste, review treatment and disposal options and boost the recovery and recycling of waste. The objective, of course, is to minimise the amount of waste going to landfill and to promote its reusability.

Packaging waste

There is a common misconception that the Packaging Waste Regulations apply to businesses who manufacture products with packaging. This is not the case. The Regulations apply to businesses which handle more than 50 tonnes of packaging in one year and whose turnover exceeds £2 million. It is the 'handling' of packaging that can most easily create confusion. A business handles packaging if it manufactures, converts, fills, sells, provides a service, imports or brings transit packaging into the UK that will end up in the UK waste stream. The definition of packaging is extremely wide and includes all products used to contain, protect, handle, deliver or present goods. It includes both returnable and non-returnable items such as boxes, palettes, labels, containers, tubes, bags and sacks. Consequently many businesses fall within the scope of the Regulations unwittingly.

The Regulations require businesses to register with their environmental regulator (in England and Wales this is the Environment Agency; in Scotland, SEPA and in Northern Ireland the Department of the Environment) annually and recycle and recover specified amounts of packaging waste calculated by reference to their turnover and the amount of packaging handled. This is a complicated calculation. Businesses can either join a registered compliance scheme or calculate their own recovery and recycling obligations. A registered compliance scheme will take on the recovery and recycling obligations of the business in return for a fee. It obtains evidence of recovery and recycling for the company by purchasing packaging waste recovery notes (PRNs) on its behalf, calculated in accordance with its packaging obligations. This is where the scheme seems slightly artificial; no actual recycling of the packaging materials needs to be carried out by the business as its compliance is satisfied by the purchase of PRN's. (The packaging materials do, however, need to be disposed of responsibly, as previously outlined.)

A business can also calculate its own recovery and recycling obligations for the coming year. To do this, it needs to know the amount of packaging and the packaging materials that were handled in the last calendar year and the activity performed on each material, together with the relevant 'percentage obligation', ie the percentage of packaging that the business needs to recover or recycle associated with each activity. Finally, the business needs to know the business recovery and recycling targets for the year. DEFRA have produced a Packaging Waste booklet which sets out in detail how these calculations are made, and their complexity should not be underestimated. There are also strict reporting requirements and consequently it appears that few businesses make their own calculations.

Small producers (those with an annual turnover of between £2 million and £5 million, which handle more than 50 tonnes of packaging per year) can choose to follow the allocation method which is a simplified process with obligations calculated simply on turnover. This method means that a business does not need to provide information to the Environment Agency about packaging handled each year, nor will it mean it has to calculate its obligations. Their obligations are satisfied by the purchase of PRN's. This method is voluntary but if a business chooses to use it they must follow it for at least 3 years.

If a business designs or produces packaging it must comply with the Essential Requirements, namely to minimise the environmental impact of the packaging, ensure that it can be reused or recycled and ensure that it does not contain high levels of heavy metals or other hazardous substances. It must keep evidence of compliance with the Essential Requirements for at least four years. Packaging produced must be recoverable through one of a number of methods such as recycling, biodegradation, composting or energy recovery.

PRN's themselves are divided into different materials covering such things as wood, plastic, paper and aluminium. PRN's are created when actual recovery and recycling of the specified materials takes place. In other words, when a quantity of, say, wood is recovered and recycled by an authorised facility it creates a PRN for that quantity which has a set value for onward sale to a business or a compliance scheme. In this way, recycling is carried, albeit not by the business itself. The targets for each specified material change annually and this does lead to a trading in PRN's on both a domestic and international basis. While the purpose of the Regulations was never to encourage a market in PRN trading this is inevitably the case where one country has failed to recycle its domestic obligation of a certain material or conversely has a surplus of PRN's in material.

Enforcement

The enforcement authorities have little time for those who breach the law on waste management either in terms of its letter or its spirit. Stories recounting the increase in fly tipping due to the heavy regulation of the waste industry are well-known. Those who deliberately flout the law will be dealt with severely and the courts are becoming more disposed to handing out heavy fines and in certain cases custodial sentences for directors of illegal operations. Fly tipping alone can prompt fines of up to £50,000.

Even less dangerous offences are attracting huge fines; in January 2008 a firm was fined £225,000 for failing to comply with the Packaging Waste Regulations. Ignorance of the Regulations is no defence and enforcement action is likely even if the offence is one 'on paper', such as failing to register with the Environment Agency. Businesses are well advised to stay abreast of developments as they can easily find themselves subject to the Regulations due to a slight change in either their turnover or packaging handled.

Conclusion

The weight of legislation regarding waste is a very real burden for industry but its purpose is both necessary and effective. Business needs to be encouraged to investigate and implement alternative methods of dealing with waste. It is not cheap or quick to deal with waste in the manner now prescribed by law, but it is needed to prevent serious environmental consequences.

There is an increasing amount of support and advice now available to businesses to assist them with compliance. This is essential: the legislation is often hard to interpret and difficult to implement. The consequences of getting it wrong are huge, both to a business' bottom line and, in a wider sense, to the environment. With targets for recycling on the increase each year it can only be assumed that waste management will soon become an obligation for all.

Rebecca Cushing is a senior assistant in the Commercial Litigation department of Field Fisher Waterhouse and a member of the cross firm environmental group. She advises on environmental disputes, environmental risk management, and health and safety issues.

Her recent work has included defending offences under the Packaging Waste Regulations, advising on EPA and water pollution claims, representing clients at interviews under caution with regulatory bodies and advising on best presentation of mitigation. She has also considered the personal liability of directors for environmental matters arising out of the new Companies Act and advised on reputational issues for companies surrounding breaches of environmental regulation.

Further details: www.ffw.com

31 Electrical waste

Rebecca Cushing at Field Fisher Waterhouse examines the implications for producers and distributors in the WEEE Directive.

The principle of 'the polluter pays' is becoming an increasing reality following the implementation into domestic law of the EC Directive on Waste Electrical and Electronic Equipment Regulations (the WEEE Regulations). Its primary aim is to address the environmental impact of electrical and electronic equipment (EEE) when it reaches the end of its natural life. The Regulations apply to all businesses, regardless of size, that manufacture, import, re-brand, distribute, sell, store, treat, dismantle, recycle, dispose and use EEE. Businesses are split into producers, distributors and end users of EEE. Producers are responsible for financing the collection, treatment and recovery of waste electrical equipment, and distributors are obliged to allow consumers to return its waste equipment to them free of charge.

With electrical waste now one of the fastest-growing waste streams across Europe – expanding at around three times the rate of general waste – the aim of the WEEE Regulations is to encourage more recycling, recovery and re-use, and ultimately divert more used goods away from landfill. Experts say that the problem is a real one. The amount of unwanted electrical waste that is thrown away is estimated as increasing by around 5% each year. This means that in one year the amount of electrical waste created in the UK could fill Wembley Stadium six times. Currently, over 75% of waste electrical goods end up in landfill where lead and other toxins contained in electrical goods can cause soil and water contamination.[1]

The Regulations came into force on 2 January 2007 and producers' responsibility for treating and recycling household WEEE began on 1 July 2007. Unsurprisingly, there are strict government targets for collection, recycling and recovery, consistent with the other Producer Responsibility Regulations.

---

1 Source: Dixons website

What is WEEE?

There are 10 categories of WEEE:

1. Large household appliances
2. Small household appliances
3. IT and telecommunications equipment
4. Consumer equipment
5. Lighting equipment
6. Electrical and electronic tools
7. Toys, leisure and sports equipment
8. Medical devices
9. Monitoring and control equipment
10. Automatic dispensers.

The Regulations apply to electrical and electronic equipment in the above categories with a voltage of up to 1000 volts AC or up to 1500 volts DC, whose main function cannot be fulfilled without the use of electricity.

WEEE products are categorised on the basis of when they were placed on to the market: those placed for sale prior to 13 August 2005 are known as 'historic products' and those after that date are called 'future products'.

Producers

A producer is a business which manufactures, imports or re-brands EEE. It is natural that some producers will also sell EEE and so will additionally be required to comply with the distributor obligations. The Regulations expect all producers to have registered with their environmental regulator by 15 March 2007, although producers cannot do this themselves but must first join a Producer Compliance Scheme (PCS), which is compulsory, which carries out the registration requirements on the producer's behalf. The role of the PCS is varied; not only do they deal with registration requirements on behalf of producers but they also manage the collection and recycling of WEEE. At this stage, the PCS provides the business with a unique producer registration number which the producer must then give to all distributors to whom it sells EEE so that they can be identified.

Producers have to bear the financial burden of collecting, treating, recovering and disposing of an equivalent amount of WEEE to the EEE which they each produce. Each producer must bear the cost of collecting, breaking down and recycling WEEE. Producers do this either through their PCS, who bears the responsibility of reporting to the regulator, or direct. If a producer wishes to do this direct it must ensure that it has, if necessary, a waste management licence and it must also ensure that the EEE recovered/recycled is taken to approved authorised treatment facilities (AATF). Whilst a producer can meet its obligations itself, if it does so, it must provide evidence to the PCS of what it has done. As can be expected the regulator is keen to monitor compliance and producers must keep evidence of their efforts for a minimum of four years.

The Regulations differentiate between household and non-household WEEE. If EEE is from household use the PCS is responsible for household WEEE collected through specific collection facilities such as civic amenity sites. The amount the PCS collects depends upon the EEE that is sold by the producer. When EEE is sold for non-household use, the PCS is responsible for collecting, treating and recycling either historic WEEE being replaced by EEE, or EEE that was sold since 13 August 2005 when it becomes WEEE.

Producers are also obligated to mark all electrical products with a crossed out wheelie bin symbol. This indicates to end users that the product should not become general waste when it reaches the end of its shelf life. As consumers become more aware generally of recycling symbols on products this will raise awareness of the re-use and recycling opportunities for such goods.

Distributors

A distributor of EEE is one who sells EEE products to end users be they business or consumer. Their obligations differ from those of producers; firstly, they must provide information to consumers and secondly, they must provide a take back scheme. The information a distributor must provide covers everything from the meaning of the crossed out wheelie bin symbol, free WEEE recycling for consumers, to why steps are being taken to eradicate WEEE. As with producers distributors must keep records of the information they produce for four years.

Whilst consumers have no obligations under the Regulations the message is clear: distributors are obliged to display information to customers on the benefits of recycling and recovery schemes so that the aim of preventing WEEE entering landfill is met from consumers as well as from businesses.

The distributor must ensure that customers can dispose of WEEE free of charge, either by way of providing an in-store take-back scheme or through a distributor take-back scheme. In either case information must be prominently displayed to encourage consumers to use these schemes. The in-store scheme ensures that a distributor must accept all types of EEE that it sells as part of the scheme and must accept waste from customers when selling them an equivalent item. The distributor must record the amount and category of items received and again keep those records safe for four years. Distributors are expected to adopt a reasonable and practical approach, the item returned may not be exactly equivalent but if it performs a similar function to the EEE purchased then it should be accepted for disposal. The distributor must then arrange for the onward removal of the WEEE collected, either through a PCS or a suitably licensed waste carrier.

The distributor take-back scheme works differently and is operated via a network of Designated Collection Facilities (DCF). Rather than collecting EEE in-store, distributors must inform consumers that they are entitled to dispose of WEEE free of charge at these facilities and explain how and where they can do this. The distributor must join and pay membership fees to the take-back scheme, currently operated by Valpak, which supports a national network of DCF's. Details of the location of local schemes can be found on www.recycle-more.co.uk.

In either case, the take back schemes are services intended to be provided to consumers free of charge. Unfortunately, in certain cases, distributors have been found to be levying a charge for the service, masking the fee as a collection rather than a disposal charge. This practice has been roundly criticised by the Environment Agency who believes it goes against the spirit of the legislation.

Even those distributors that operate through mail order or internet sales must still provide a take-back scheme, either by joining the distributor take-back scheme or providing a collection from home scheme.

Business as end user

All businesses that use EEE are required also to comply with the Regulations when managing their WEEE. Businesses must obtain and keep proof that WEEE was given to a waste management company and was treated and disposed of in an environmentally sound way when removing WEEE from site.

WEEE can be returned free of charge to the producer if it was sold to the business after 13 August 2005 and it is being replaced with new equivalent EEE. In those circumstances the producer's PCS is responsible for the WEEE and the distributor from whom the EEE was purchased can give the end-user information on the take-back scheme available. However, the business must arrange and pay for WEEE to be transferred to an approved authorised treatment facility if it is being discarded, was purchased prior to 13 August 2005 and is not being replaced with equivalent EEE.

Enforcement

As with all Producer Responsibility Regulations enforcement is taken very seriously. Under the WEEE Regulations enforcement is split between the

VCA, which deals with EEE distributor obligations and the wheelie bin product marking of new EEE, and the Environment Agency, which predominantly deals with producer obligations and DCF/PCS operators.

Whilst the emphasis will be on assisting businesses to comply, the ability to prosecute does exist and will be exercised where offenders have knowingly or recklessly breached the Regulations. Prosecution is a very wide ranging and invasive power that businesses are well advised to avoid. Enforcement officers have extensive powers of entry and inspection. They also have the ability to question individuals suspected of committing an offence. If businesses are found guilty of an offence under the Regulations they may be liable to a fine of up to £5,000 in a magistrates' court, but if the case is heard in a Crown Court, the fine is unlimited. Directors may also be prosecuted in a personal capacity.

Conclusion

The Environment Agency estimates that the amount of WEEE hitting landfill sites prior to the introduction of the Regulations approached 2 million tonnes in the UK and a very real problem existed, particularly in an age of sophisticated EEE product development and market competition. Implicit in this is a drive for producers to improve the environmental performance and longevity of their products. Initial indications show that businesses are taking their responsibilities seriously and there are no reported cases of prosecution under the Regulations to date. It will take time for the full impact of the Regulations to be felt and some confusion inevitably still exists over who takes what WEEE from whom. The cost of these obligations to business is still also unclear, but until the scheme has been in use for some time, one can only hope that its achievements will be considered as laudable as its aims.

Rebecca Cushing is a senior assistant in the Commercial Litigation department of Field Fisher Waterhouse and a member of the cross firm environmental group. She advises on environmental disputes, environmental risk management, and health and safety issues.

Her recent work has included defending offences under the Packaging Waste Regulations, advising on EPA and water pollution claims, representing clients at interviews under caution with regulatory bodies and advising on best presentation of mitigation. She has also considered the personal liability of directors for environmental matters arising out of the new Companies Act and advised on reputational issues for companies surrounding breaches of environmental legislation.

Further details: www.ffw.com

Part 7

Transport

32 Travel plans

Dr Colin Black, ACT TravelWise Director, discusses how to reduce your CO_2 through travel planning.

What is a travel plan?

Travel plans first emerged in the UK in the mid 1990s and aim to promote sustainable travel to work, and travel at work, by offering realistic transport choices. Travel Plans are not 'anti-car', but emphasise the travel choices that are available and offer practical measures on how to improve accessibility for everyone. Each organisation's travel plan is individually tailored to address the particular needs of its employees and site location.

Initially, organisations developed travel plans voluntarily to tackle rising congestion, pollution and parking problems on site. With subsequent changes to national planning policy, travel plans are now integrated into most new developments and many businesses are beginning to embrace the wider benefits of having a travel plan – either as a voluntary gesture or via a compulsory planning condition.

Why have a travel plan?

Travel is the one thing that unites people – most employees have to travel to various degrees every single day. There are numerous good business motivations for implementing a travel plan that range from cost savings, HR benefits (in terms of recruitment and retention, as well as reduced sickness absence) and improving the corporate image.

The environment

It is the environmental agenda that is at the top of the list for many organisations. Congestion and air pollution are still as important to tackle today as they were a decade ago, but in recent years environmental protection has become not only an acceptable reason to take action, but seen as an urgent responsibility to share. It is now widely accepted that climate change is happening, and any organisation lacking plans to mitigate climate change and adapt to the effects of it could be seen to be irresponsible in the eyes of its customers. An active travel plan will help cut CO_2 emissions by reducing unnecessary car trips, improving fuel efficiency and promoting 'smarter working' to eliminate the need to travel at all. In terms of adaptation, changing the culture of an organisation can now reduce its dependence on the car further down the line, providing more flexibility to continue business operations in our changing climate.

In recognition of the important role travel plans have to play in reducing CO_2 emissions, a novel carbon footprinting tool has been developed to help organisations measure, monitor and minimise their travel carbon footprint. YETI (Yearly Emissions from Travel Information) is a freely available, web-based tool to facilitate and promote inclusion of transport in corporate reports. For more information visit www.smarterchoices.co.uk.

Financial

Fuels are a finite resource, and as stocks get lower market forces dictate that the price of oil is going to increase. This will directly impact on business as operations become more costly, particularly in sectors that rely heavily on travel and transportation. Improvements in engine and fuel technology will evolve, and a travel plan can embrace these (along with other technological solutions such as satellite navigation to cut unnecessary mileage). Despite this, it is even more effective to stop wasting fuel by replacing short journeys by car with walking and cycling, and making greater use of train services for longer distance (especially inter city) journeys. In the latter case, employees can be more productive on the train by working or resting, rather than sitting in queues of traffic getting stressed.

Carbon trading and climate change levies are already being imposed on companies to encourage a reduction in their energy consumption. Currently this doesn't extend to transport, but, with the release of novel reporting tools like YETI, this is only a matter of time. On top of other cost savings, a travel plan could instigate change in the organisation to reduce energy consumption in transport ahead of the introduction of any new levy.

Corporate social responsibility

It's difficult to measure the impact of corporate activity, but it's generally accepted that many consumers are influenced by the ethical credentials of an organisation. The green agenda has boomed in recent years, almost to the point that consumers are cynical that organisations are 'jumping on the band wagon' without any real understanding or commitment to the principles of environmental management. A travel plan fits in well with accredited environmental schemes, such as ISO14001 or EMAS. Far from being 'greenwash', these management systems are respected and bring a wealth of other benefits besides the glowing company image. Some organisations have already developed and implemented procurement policies which demand such environmental credentials from a supplier before they are willing to do business. Could you lose business to such a client?

How do I implement a travel plan in my organisation?

A travel plan should aim to reduce traffic levels to and on your site, and address any specific problems or issues that car dependency is causing for your organisation. Before any travel plan can be developed and implemented you need firm management commitment from the senior levels of the organisation, and to involve employees across all functions in order to get 'buy in' at all levels.

There are three main aspects that can be tackled: the commute, business travel and smarter working.

The commute

Whilst employees technically commute in their own time, there are still 'carrot and stick' initiatives that can be employed by a company to influence the way individuals get to the workplace.

The following is a 'shopping list' of travel plan elements for consideration:

Promotion of non-car modes

- Provision of adequate lighting, convenient footpaths and site access points for cyclists and pedestrians

- Provision of personal alarms to staff

- Provision of on-site security.

- Provision of walking and cycling maps.

- Provision of covered, 'Sheffield stand' style cycle parking (for staff and visitors)

- Provision of changing/storage facilities for cyclists and motorcycle users

- Creation of a Bicycle User Group

- Provision of Pool bikes

- Cycle mileage payments

- Active dissemination of public transport information

- Interest free loans for season tickets

- Discounted public transport travel

- Company shuttle bus/works bus

- Financial incentives for public transport users

- Public transport, cycling and walking information on staff/public/ visitor notice board.

Car parking and car sharing

- Car parking restraint (barriers/permits/charging) and management

- Provision of dedicated car-share spaces

- Guaranteed 'get you home' service for stranded car sharers

- Financial incentives for car-sharers

- Financial incentives to staff giving up a car parking space.

Business travel

Some organisations undertake a considerable amount of miles carrying out day to day business functions. The rising costs of fuel make this an obvious area to scrutinise in order to improve efficiency. Furthermore, a commute journey by car is often intrinsically linked to the need to have the car available for business journeys. A travel plan can incorporate some of the following elements to assist management of at-work travel:

- Pool vehicles (preferably vehicles with good environmental credentials)

- Correct choice of fuel type for the intended use – including petrol, diesel, LPG, and hybrid electric.

- Restructuring of company car policy

- Restructuring of business mileage rates

- Promotion of public transport for business travel

- Sustainable fleet management policy

- Driver training.

Smarter working

Finally, perhaps the most environmentally sound mile is the one not travelled at all, so using Human Resources policies and technology to reduce the need to travel can reduce carbon emissions and improve the bottom line. A travel plan could consider:

- Flexible working practices, such as flexible start and finish times and flexi-days.

- Flexible working practices, such as hot desking at the nearest office

- Working from home

- Local recruitment policy to prioritise those living within walking and cycling distance

- Tele/video/web conferencing to connect up offices

- Introduction of a compressed working week (e.g. full-time hours compressed into four days)

- Provision of on-site facilities (banking / canteen etc).

Additionally, marketing the plan should be a consideration as there is little point spending time and energy setting up schemes and policies if nobody gets to hear about them. Regular monitoring (every 1–3 years) is also essential, so a programme of staff travel surveys to record any reductions in car dependency is a good thing to incorporate in the plan.

ACT TravelWise is an organisation that provides training, advice and support for businesses to develop travel plans. See www.acttravelwise.org for details.

Your County Council or Local Authority may also have a 'travel plan officer' who can give advice on travel plans, and sometimes funding and grants are available to help with elements of a travel plan.

33 Alternative fuels for vehicles

Noel Lock at Greenfuel reviews the relative merits of bio, gas and electric.

Opinion is divided as to the extent that humans are currently damaging the planet and the future consequences of this. Also, there are some that insist that 'Peak Oil' is upon us and others that argue that reserves of oil will keep going for a considerable period yet.

There is however, broad consensus that the public is increasingly concerned about the environment and more likely to factor this in to their buying behaviour and that oil, and consequently petrol and diesel, have become increasingly expensive and are likely to remain so.

There are, therefore, two good reasons for fleets to consider the use of alternative fuels; image, CSR, brand, call it what you will, and the prerogative to drive down costs.

There are several different alternative fuels available or planned, and it is essential to understand that no single alternative is a 'silver bullet' to solve the world's road fuel needs but that as a collective they can, and will, make an increasingly important contribution. So here is my effort at giving a brief outline of the fuels available and their suitable uses. I have not included low-blend bio-fuels as legislation is in place to ensure that they replace pure petrol/diesel shortly anyway (Renewable Transport Fuels Obligation – RTFO).

Biofuels

The main attraction of high-blend or pure Bio-diesel or SVO (straight vegetable oil) is that they are made from a renewable resource that actually captures CO_2 during its production, thereby claiming to be carbon neutral in a 'well-to-wheel' or 'earth-to-engine' sense.

Fuel cost is based on a number of factors, material costs, economies of scale, tax treatment, etc. I have based my cost assessment on the assumption that the user is a commercial fleet, so, for example, B100 (high blend bio-diesel) and SVO (straight vegetable oil) is likely to be as expensive as the reduced tax will be covered by the increased material costs, though this may change as oil prices continue to rise. Individuals have the advantage of using these fuels without paying any tax.

The great controversy with Bio-fuels is the sourcing of materials. There is a unified view that cutting down rainforest to plant bio-fuel crops is an environmental disaster that simply makes global warming much worse. There is also much concern that fuel production will displace food production. It is hoped that new bio-fuels from such sources as algae will eliminate this problem. In any case, these arguments put a case for controls and regulations rather then argue against bio-fuels themselves. The concept of turning waste into fuel is attractive but creates problems with quality consistency and will probably turn out to have niche rather than general application.

Currently there are three main inhibiting factors to the fleet use of high-blend bio-fuels, these being lack of refuelling infrastructure, lack of OEM approved vehicles and lack of financial incentive to adopt. Despite this, there are a number of fleets, notably some councils and supermarket chains, that are successfully adopting this technology with at least one impressive solution provider in the UK. Key factors to consider are the level of vehicle modifications required, the practicality of bunkering fuel and ensuring a supply of fuel of a consistent quality. Fuel bunkering favours vehicles that have a return to base scope of operations but the vehicles will retain the ability to operate on mineral diesel, and vehicle performance and range will remain the same (or be enhanced in the case of separate tanks for the bio-fuel). Currently, however, adoption of these fuels may achieve our first objective but will not drive down operating costs. This is largely due to tax treatment and is consequently subject to changing political will.

Gaseous fuels

LPG (Liquefied petroleum gas), CNG (Compressed Natural Gas) and Hydrogen all offer local air quality benefits. Sixteen million people in the UK cook with an open flame natural gas cooker in their kitchen and a quick glance at the underside of a saucepan will testify to its clean burning. Hydrogen offers the prospect of a complete elimination of toxic emissions.

LPG benefits from low taxation and consequently a cost advantage, a nation-wide refuelling infrastructure and abundant domestic production (the UK is Europe's largest producer at over six million tonnes per annum, enough for over six million vehicles). LPG vehicles retain the ability to run on petrol and typically the LPG tank is put in the place of a spare wheel. LPG is becoming a very popular fuel for the benefits described. Globally there are now over 14 million LPG vehicles with Germany being one of the fastest growing markets on the strength of long-term government commitments.

Unfortunately, there is a limited choice of OEM vehicles so the majority are aftermarket conversions. This means that there is an upfront cost and warranty issues. In the UK there is a workshop approval scheme run by the UKLPG Association and a small number of companies capable of providing UK-wide fleet support. LPG is still a fossil fuel, albeit a by-product.

CNG is an even cleaner fuel than LPG but requires heavier tanks and is therefore more suitable for larger vehicles. A lack of refuelling infrastruc-ture indicates a return to base vehicle operation. An excellent application of this fuel would be to capture the methane given off by landfill sites and use it to fuel the refuse trucks that operate from them (releasing unburnt methane has a bigger effect on climate change than burning it leading to the scientifically sound but politically unpopular view that a cow is more damaging than a Range Rover).

Hydrogen is currently not a practical fuel for vehicles and will remain so for the foreseeable future. This is despite the fact that there are some demon-stration vehicles in operation (London has three hydrogen buses). Hydrogen has some major cost issues to overcome before it can be considered for wide-spread application, very much mirroring space tourism. Equally, sustainable power generation needs to reach far greater technological heights before it becomes environmentally sound.

Electric

Vehicles that rely entirely on electric motors are extremely good for local air quality and are also quieter. Their performance is currently limited, restricting their use to milk float type operations. Increased electrical demand currently necessitates power generation through fossil fuel so in terms of mitigating climate change the verdict on electric vehicles is dependant on new sustainable power generation.

Hybrid vehicles such as the Toyota Prius are an excellent technological solution as the electrical power is derived from regenerative braking (like a bicycle dynamo), a source of energy that is wasted on most vehicles. When power demand is low such as in urban traffic the vehicle, running solely on electric motors, emits no toxic emissions and obviously population centres are where air quality is most important. However, the added weight of the hybrid system and the smaller engine count against vehicles such as the Prius on motorway runs where they will emit more CO_2 than efficient diesel vehicles.

The table opposite summarises the main options available.

The extent to which a company will adopt alternative fuels will be dictated by their enthusiasm to be seen to be 'green' and to drive down costs. Many will understandably want a 'blue chip' (ie established oil company and car manufacturer) solution. Unfortunately, this limits options and companies with this approach may find that they fall behind more pro-active companies in this field.

The good news is that there are already a variety of options available now and that these will only increase in the coming years. My advice is not to wait for the 'winner' to emerge because there will be no 'silver bullet' solution. Rather explore the possibilities now and choose the most appropriate for your vehicle type and usage.

	B100	E85	SVO	LPG	CNG	Hydrogen	Electric	Hybrid
Fuel Cost	Same	Higher	Same	Lower	Lower	Higher	Lower	Lower
Renewable	Yes	Yes	Yes	No	No	N/A	Depends	No
CO2	Better	Better	Better	Better	Better	Worse	Worse	Better
Air Quality	Same	Same	Same	Better	Better	Excellent	Excellent	Better
Refuelling Infrastructure	No	No	No	Yes	No	No	Yes	Yes
Vehicle Modification	Yes	Yes	Yes	Yes	Yes	Yes	No	No
Dualfuel/Flexfuel	Yes	Yes	Yes	Yes	Yes	Sometimes	No	Yes
Suitability	Modified diesel vehicles	Modified petrol vehicles	Modified diesel vehicles	Modified petrol vehicles	Modified Large vehicles	Unknown	Low performance criteria	Modified vehicles all base fuels
OEM Available	No	Limited	No	Limited	No	No	Limited	Limited

Noel Lock is a founder and director of the Greenfuel Company. The Greenfuel Company was founded to reduce harmful pollutants and emissions across the UK through both the promotion and the provision of practical and cost effective ways of making vehicles cleaner. To date the company's principal activities have been in the conversion of cars and vans to LPG. The company hope to announce successful completion of bio-fuel trials in the latter half of 2008.

Noel Lock, The Greenfuel Company Ltd, Monkton Combe, Bath BA2 7HY Tel: 01225 722610 Fax: 01225 723876 Email: noel.lock@greenfuel.org.uk Web: http://www.greenfuel.org.uk/

34 Green fleets

Nigel Underdown, head of transport at the Energy Saving Trust, says that business in the UK could save £3 billion a year by running its fleets in a more environmentally friendly fashion.

Environmental issues and energy efficiency in particular, have risen dramatically up the business agenda for organisations of all sizes over the past year. We have seen a phenomenal rise in the number of companies approaching the Energy Saving Trust for support, input and counsel in their efforts to help them and their customers in 'going green'.

In the past year, the Energy Saving Trust has worked with the likes of Lloyds Bank, Sainsbury's, Royal Sun Alliance and Vodaphone, amongst others. When companies of this size and standing are making a commitment in this area the message is clear: climate change is a real issue for business and it's here to stay.

We all need to work together to ensure that activity being undertaken is resulting in real carbon reductions. This is where organisations such as the Energy Saving Trust come in as we are well placed to help ensure that the advice we give and the actions we recommend to consumers or businesses is impartial, independent and given with the sole aim of delivering those savings.

Those companies and organisations that are truly committed to tackling their own carbon footprint take a 360 degree view on where those savings can be made throughout the organisation. Company car fleets contribute a significant amount of carbon dioxide emissions – around half of new cars registered each year are for business purposes.

The initial reaction from many when developing a greener fleet is that it will cost them money. Yet, our calculations for the launch of our transport report 'Behind the Wheel' in 2007 showed that UK businesses could save £3 billion a year by running their fleets in a more environmentally friendly fashion.

Encouragingly, the Energy Saving Trust's Green Fleet Review programme has seen a huge rise in interest from businesses and organisations wishing to reduce their fleet's carbon emissions – there has been a 100% increase in uptake of green fleet reviews since 2005. The Motorvate programme, which verifies companies carbon reductions from their fleets and can be used as part of ISO 14001 accreditation, was successfully relaunched in 2007.

Additionally, the Energy Saving Trust's Fleet Heroes Awards in 2007, set up to recognise the efforts of companies and organisations' efforts in reducing their fleets' carbon emissions, saw a surge of entries from companies and organisation of all sizes. Winners included Whitbread plc, Sainsbury's Online and London Borough of Islington.

Looking forward to the year to come, early indicators are positive: research from our follow up business transport report, 'Behind the Wheel II', shows that there has been a significant rise in companies developing CSR or environmental policies and, further more, including their fleets' emissions in those policies. In November 2006, the findings revealed that fewer than half of the companies surveyed (48%) have CSR or environmental policies, and of those only 42 per cent of companies take into consideration the impact of their vehicles on the environment.

In November 2007, these figures had risen slightly to 49 percent of companies with environmental or CSR policies and an encouraging 57 per cent of those companies had incorporated their fleets' emissions into those policies – demonstrating that companies are beginning to seriously address business transport.

There is no right way or wrong way to reducing a company's business transport emissions; what works for one company may not for another, but all companies can employ a variety of solutions that will lead to successful carbon emission reductions. 'Behind the Wheel II' looks at the different challenges affecting different areas of business and industry, and how a green fleet is complimentary to their green endeavours in other areas of the their operation.

Funded through the Department for Transport, the Energy Saving Trust offers a free **green fleet review** consultancy service to companies with over 50 vehicles in England and 20 vehicles in Scotland, which is funded through the Scottish Government. For companies with 20 – 49 vehicles the Energy Saving Trust offers a free telephone consultancy service.

The Energy Saving Trust also runs the **Motorvate club** on behalf of the Department for Transport. This is an accreditation scheme that sets measurable carbon reduction targets for companies who wish to demonstrate their commitment to lowering their carbon dioxide emissions and receive certification from an independent, respected source.

Advice and material on running green fleets is available from: www.energysavingtrust.org.uk/fleet or calling 0845 602 1425.

Top tips for greener fleet management

1   Promote cars with low CO_2 emissions to reduce employee car tax and National Insurance.

2   Evaluate alternative fuel cars to see if they might benefit your fleet.

3   Ensure vehicles are regularly serviced – poorly maintained vehicles have higher toxic emissions and fuel consumption.

4   Identify opportunities to reduce mileage by recording and analysing business travel.

5   Record and analyse individual fuel consumption to encourage fuel efficient driving.

6   Promote safe, economic and environmentally friendly driver training.

7   Ensure mileage reimbursement rates are environmentally sensitive and do not encourage drivers to make excessive journeys.

8   Provide access to websites and route planners to minimise vehicle mileage.

9   Promote satellite navigation and telematics to help drivers avoid congestion and use the most efficient route to reach their destination.

10   Review arrangements for tele/video conferencing as an alternative to business travel.

For further information on how the Energy Saving Trust can help support your business in making its fleet more environmentally friendly call 0845 602 1425 or visit www.energysavingtrust.org.uk/fleet

Part 8

Green buildings

35 Zero carbon development

Buildings are a major source of emissions in their own right.
Sarah Youren at Field Fisher Waterhouse examines how their
carbon impact is going to move to zero.

*"The UK emitted more than 550 million tonnes of carbon dioxide in 2005.
Energy use in buildings accounted for nearly half of these emissions and
more than a quarter came from the energy we use to heat, light and run
our homes."*

This startling quote comes from the government's policy statement
'Building a Greener Future' and goes some way towards explaining the
latest push to create zero carbon development to minimize our future impact
on the environment.

What does zero carbon actually mean?

There has been much debate about what zero carbon actually means.
Should it simply encompass energy use within a building once that building
has been constructed? Alternatively, should it also include the energy used
in the construction process, including transporting the materials to site
and physically constructing the building? Or, as the hard line environmentalists would prefer, should it include every aspect of the building
including the energy cost of creating the materials from which the building
is constructed.

The Government has decided that in relation to new build residential at
least, zero carbon will mean that "over a year, the net carbon emissions
from all energy use in the home will be zero".

For new non-domestic buildings zero carbon will mean that the net actual
carbon emissions from a new building are zero over a year, taking account
of typical behaviour. The definition does not include the overall building
carbon footprint, such as links between the building and transport

networks, logistics, water use, embodied energy and construction energy. In terms of energy use within a building it will include use of electronic equipment in offices and use of refrigeration in supermarkets. It will not include energy used for industrial processes, lifetime carbon impact of technologies, ie the emissions associated with manufacture as well as use, transport emissions, actual behaviour of people occupying the buildings, green tarrifs, offsetting.

Who will the new rules apply to?

1. New build residential development

New homes currently make up less than 1% of the housing stock, however, the Government has calculated that if we build the number of homes that it is anticipated that we will need in the UK to cope with predicted levels of demand, then by 2050 as much as one third of the total housing stock will be post 2008 buildings. This is the rationale for making more stringent changes to new build than to existing housing stock. The sheer amount of new housing required should make it worthwhile to invest in developing new environmental technology and produce economies of scale to reduce the cost, thereby enabling it to also be introduced in existing housing stock.

Changes to building regulations

For new build residential development the Government proposes to improve the energy/carbon performance set out in part L of the Building Regulations with a view to achieving zero carbon housing within ten years. This will be done in three steps. Firstly, a 25% improvement in 2010 compared to 2006 Part L Building Regulations. Secondly, a 44% improvement in 2013 and then zero carbon in 2016.[1] The Government believes that achieving this target will save a least 15 million tonnes of carbon dioxide emissions per year by 2050. The changes will involve strengthening the requirements in relation to insulation, ventilation, air tightness, heating and lighting fittings.

---

1 Building a Greener Future: Policy Statement

Changes to the planning regime

At the same time the Government has published PPS1 on climate change which encourages the setting of a framework for development to achieve zero carbon outcomes. PPS1 states that all new development should take account of landform, layout, building orientation, massing and landscaping to minimise energy consumption, including maximising cooling and avoiding solar gain in the summer, and be planned so as to minimise carbon dioxide emissions by looking at how all aspects of development form together with the density and mix of development, support opportunities for decentralised and renewable or low carbon energy supply. The Government has also announced its intention to work with industry and organisations such as English Partnerships to encourage exemplar developments.

Code for Sustainable Homes

The Government has also just published the final version of the Code for Sustainable Homes. This is a voluntary code which is intended to promote higher environmental standards in housing in advance of regulatory standards. It considers energy/carbon and also other sustainability issues such as water, waste and materials. Whilst the code itself remains voluntary, the Government is considering requiring all new homes to be rated against the code to demonstrate the level of environmental standards reached.

Stamp duty relief

To encourage development of zero carbon homes the Government has also announced that it will introduce a time limited stamp duty land tax relief with effect from 1 October 2007, for new homes built to a zero carbon standard. If the sale price is £500,000 or less then no stamp duty will be payable. If the sale price is more than £500,000 stamp duty will be reduced by £15,000. It only applies to the first sale of the property however, so subsequent purchasers will not benefit.

Construction of zero carbon homes will undoubtedly cost more than conventional homes, however, for the occupier there will be benefits in terms of lower fuel bills and warmer houses in the winter months.

2. Existing residential development

Energy Performance Certificates are currently being phased in. These will provide buyers with detailed information about the energy performance of their home together with a report on actions they can take to reduce carbon emissions and lower their fuel bills. It is too early yet to tell whether this information will have any great effect on the decision-making process of potential buyers.

3. Commercial development

Measuring energy performance for non-domestic buildings is complex. The diversity of the non-domestic building stock, with differing sizes of units and styles of buildings from small kiosks to large single storey sheds to tall office blocks, poses challenges in measuring and comparing energy efficiency. The range of activities accommodated within non-domestic buildings is huge from occasional community use to full-time care homes. A further complication is the use of buildings by several occupiers who may have multiple sources of heating and cooling, and differing levels of intensity of use.

Anticipated timescale for carbon reductions

Nonetheless, the Government has stated that it is also vitally important that new commercial development addresses the challenges posed by climate change. They believe it should be technically and economically possible for all new non-domestic buildings to achieve substantial reductions in carbon emissions over the next decade, and anticipate that many such buildings may be able to achieve zero carbon on non-process related emissions. Buildings outside dense urban centres and those with low appliance energy requirements, such as warehouses, distribution centres and some retail outlets, should be able to be built to a zero carbon specification in a shorter time scale than other building types. The Government is working closely with industry to learn from existing exemplar developments to understand the costs involved and the barriers to progress. The intention is to set in place a clear timetable and action plan to deliver substantial reductions in carbon emissions from new commercial buildings within the next ten years. It is likely that changes will then be made to the building regulations.

Barriers to zero carbon

The Government is also conducting a review of the sustainability of existing non-domestic stock to identify the measures that can be taken to improve their performance, the barriers that prevent owners and occupiers taking action, and the most effective policy instruments that could be used to overcome these barriers.

Energy Performance Certificates

In the meantime Energy Performance Certificates on the sale and letting of non-domestic buildings will be start being phased in. They will apply to commercial buildings with a floor area of more than 10,000 square metres from 6 April 2008, to commercial buildings with a floor area of more than 25,000 square metres from 1 July 2008 and for all commercial buildings from 1 October 2008. The occupier will also be given a report detailing the improvements to the building that the assessor recommends should be carried out in order to improve the buildings energy performance. This may well prove to be a negotiation point on sales, new lettings and rent reviews.

The Carbon Reduction Commitment

The Government announced in the Energy White Paper that it would introduce a mandatory UK cap and trade scheme called the Carbon Reduction Commitment focussed on large commercial and public sector organisations to secure further savings of 4.4 million tonnes of carbon dioxide emissions per year in 2020. These will apply to organisations rather than to buildings, however, it should provide an incentive for large non-energy intensive organisations to reduce carbon emissions from their own buildings.

How much responsibility should the occupier have?

The UK Green Building Council (an industry led, not for profit, membership-based organisation) published a report in December 2007 on carbon reductions in new non-domestic buildings. This report highlighted the fact that whilst Energy Performance Certificates state the energy efficiency that the building should enjoy, in fact much depends on the behaviour of the occupier of the building. The UKGBC believed that at current energy prices there is little incentive on the occupier to reduce energy demand, and they proposed that the Government should give consideration to requiring the occupier to pay for the actual amount of carbon emitted (as shown by the Display Energy Certificate) above the amount predicted to be used in the building by the Energy Performance Certificate. It remains to be seen whether the Government will take up this suggestion.

How do you achieve zero carbon development?

The definition of zero carbon development includes energy use throughout the year from appliances within the home or office. This means that developers will have to explore zero and low carbon sources of electricity supply which is an area that is currently outside the control of Building Regulations. For most developers this will be a new area requiring new technical skills and understanding of a new regulatory system.

The Government has made it clear that solutions to zero carbon for both domestic and non-domestic buildings are acceptable at the development level, rather than for each individual unit. Development-wide solutions such as district heating, combined heat and power or a wind turbine producing energy for the whole development site for example, could be used to meet the requirements.

For residential development the Government has stated that any type of technology that has a physical connection to the development, even if the technology is wholly or partly located away from the development site itself will be acceptable. The Standard Assessment Procedure will be updated to take account of this type of technology.

For non-domestic buildings the Government is encouraging developers to look at introducing more efficient systems, fabric improvements, passive cooling, better control systems, better building management, building level low and zero carbon technologies, and development level low and zero carbon technologies. Only if it is clear that these are not delivering the necessary carbon reductions or that the cost is disproportionate, will it be acceptable to look at low and zero carbon technologies away from the development.

Rising to the challenge

Some companies, such as Zed Homes, are already rising to the zero carbon challenge by focussing their entire business strategy on building low and zero carbon developments.

Ashford Borough Council has teamed up with Hyde Housing Association to create a zero carbon affordable housing scheme. Ashford Borough Council executive portfolio holder for housing, Councillor Peter Wood, said: "This exemplar housing scheme would place Ashford at the forefront of environmentally sustainable development and present a beacon of excellence for other local authorities and housing developers."

In London, BioRegional Quintain and Crest Nicholson are developing a zero carbon scheme at Gallions Park. They are employing a host of measures including renewable energy, energy efficient architecture, natural materials, integrated waste management, onsite food growing and green transport measures such as car and cycle clubs.

Sarah is a partner in the Planning and Environment team at Field Fisher Waterhouse. She advises on all aspects of planning and environmental law from inception to construction of a project. Her clients include private developers, funders, local authorities and Government organisations.

The Planning and Environment team advise on all aspects of planning and environmental law. We have a particular interest in sustainable development and help clients obtain planning permission, evaluate Environmental Impact Assessments, negotiate planning and infrastructure agreements and acquire sites through compulsory purchase. On the environmental side we offer skilled and commercial advice on issues such as flooding, contaminated land, waste, water pollution and recycling. We have considerable experience in the energy field and with flood related development.

Further details: www.ffw.com

36 Green buildings

"Your place of work should be at the forefront of the fight against climate change", argues Paul King, Chief Executive of the UK Green Building Council.

In the last year or two it has become hard not to open a newspaper or turn on the TV without coming across phrases like 'carbon footprint' and 'sustainability'. Environmental issues, in particular climate change, have risen up the media, political and, of course, business agenda. This is a positive step forward, but there is a plethora of advice on how to 'go green', some of which is confusing.

It's worth stepping back for a moment and remembering that climate change is undoubtedly the most urgent threat we face as a planet, and the science gets ever more compelling. Drought, extreme weather and species loss add up to an environmental and humanitarian disaster, unless we act fast.

Buildings account for about 50% of the UK's total greenhouse gas emissions, and the production of materials used in buildings accounts for a further 10%. Buildings are also major consumers of water, timber and other materials – so they have a massive impact not just on our contribution to climate change, but other environmental problems, both in the UK and around the world.

This can be quite overwhelming, and there is a real danger that 'doom and gloom' scenarios create a sense of hopelessness and defeatism. However, I believe we have to treat the challenge of climate change as an opportunity, rather than a threat. Nowhere is this challenge greater than in the business community.

The focus of the media tends to be on the big, often global, businesses – the BPs, the Toyotas, the HSBCs – and their much publicised green initiatives. Much less attention is focussed on small and medium-sized businesses and the efforts they have taken, or should be taking to reduce their impact on the environment.

Easy wins

Energy efficiency is an attractive energy source in itself, says Beatrice Otto, a leading sustainable designer. It is universally available, it is under-exploited and it is relatively cheap. Here she offers some general pointers:

- **Ban the bulb**. Lighting uses about 17% of global power consumption and that's only what it takes for an incandescent bulb to turn energy into light at a paltry conversion rate of 5%. A lot of the other 95% generates heat which ramps up the cooling costs of buildings. Go for the low-energy long-life successors, including LEDs where appropriate.

- **Dim the switch**. By giving employees more individual control of lighting, energy use drops. In aggregate, people seem to choose lower levels of artificial light than standard facility design suggests. Being able to work at their own comfort level also tends to improve well-being and productivity.

- **Day light**. Ban the bulb also through natural lighting. There is burgeoning evidence that this reduces not only energy consumption, but employee fatigue, headaches and error rates. Consequently, energy savings can be dwarfed by gains in productivity and concomitant well-being. If that isn't enough, some retailers have found natural lighting increases sales. There are many ways to do this, from removing curtains to installing light shelves, which transmit light from the edge to the interior in a diffused, eye-friendly way, and light pipes, which look like ceiling lamps but are sun-lit.

- **Seize the trees**. A tree planted in a built up area can have a stronger effect on reducing climate impacts by lowering ambient temperatures and providing shade, reducing cooling loads. Other simple things to reduce the 'urban heat island' effect include using paler paving or roofing, and using water features to provide a cooling effect through evaporation.

- **Revisit the shop floor.** An energy efficiency guru flipped the usual process for designing a factory. Instead of putting in the machinery, then connecting the pipes, he did it the other way around. Lay out the pipes first, with as few kinks and corners as possible, thereby reducing friction and the size of the motors needed, and watch the energy plummet. He also went for bigger pipes, again to reduce friction, so needing smaller motors.

- **Don't stand for stand-by.** 'Stand-by' is a posh word for 'idling'. It uses masses of energy pointlessly. Encourage employees to switch off the computer when they go home, and to unplug their mobile chargers when idle.

- **Reduce the use.** Energy efficiency can also come from reduced material inputs, or using recycled materials. Recycling aluminium uses 95% less energy than producing it from scratch – an obvious big gain, but don't be fooled into thinking that recycled is always better. This addresses 'embedded energy' – the type that doesn't show up on your own energy bills.

- **Logical logistics.** Similarly, don't get hooked on what seems an impact-lite material or component without considering the transport involved. The less than perfect product next door might be a better option than the dream-green item that's been shipped or trucked five times around the globe.

Further details: Beatrice Otto is the author of the Design Council's expert article on Sustainable Design (http://www.designcouncil.org.uk/en/About-Design/Business-Essentials/Sustainability/).

But it is down to all of us, whether CEOs of multinationals, owners of one or two person businesses, or executives in medium-sized companies – as well as individuals in our own lives – to take the steps we can to help in the fight against climate change. A company doesn't have to be involved in directly burning fossil fuels as their core business to have an impact.

Almost all companies own or occupy buildings (or work out of a home office), and these should be at the forefront of strategies to reduce energy use.

Businesses that save energy also save money – so there is a bottom line incentive to act. Of course, the theory is often harder to put into practice, but there are a number of good ways forward. The first thing to consider is that all employees should be aware of the need to put in place a carbon management strategy. Education is very important. Buy-in from colleagues will only be achieved with full communication and shared understanding. Subscribing to a magazine like Sustainable Business or Green Futures is a good way to keep informed on best practice and current debates – and there is no substitute for genuinely spreading enthusiasm and encouraging all employees to take responsibility.

Before planning how to improve, companies obviously need to measure what their current impact is. How this is done will depend on the size of the company, their day-to-day practices and the size of the building they occupy. A starting point is reading energy and water meters. If there aren't any – put them in! Understanding energy use should be made easier in due course as the Government roles out Energy Performance Certificates and Display Energy Certificates, giving information on how energy efficient our homes and buildings are and including advice on what can be done to improve them.

It's important to manage properties professionally, maintaining heating and air-con systems properly. Get the landlord to do it too – it's actually a health and safety requirement. The list of simple actions that can be taken is almost endless. Everyday practices – the 'low hanging fruit' – include recycling of waste including electrical equipment, composting rubbish where appropriate, switching off equipment and not leaving on stand-by, always printing double-sided and on scrap if for draft use and so on. Try setting the thermostat, or equivalent, a bit lower in winter and a bit higher in summer if possible.

Another measure that can deliver major carbon savings is a staff travel plan – encouraging staff to walk, cycle, car-share or use public transport. Can free bikes be made available? Are there shower facilities in the work-place? Is it feasible or appropriate to put on a shuttle bus? This can be made into a positive staff benefit, as colleagues save money by sharing lifts, experience less traffic congestion around busy workplaces, and feel fitter and healthier as a result of their choices.

Other important questions to ask: Do the offices have double glazing? Are they properly insulated? Install a mains water cooler instead of trucking water around. Talk to the landlord and see what the options are. When re-fitting an office, there are a whole host of fantastic and high quality products, such as table tops made from recycled plastic and flooring made from recycled materials. When buying wood products, make sure it's FSC-certified timber. Don't be tempted into tokenism, such as installing a micro-wind turbine for the sake of it, take advice from experts to determine how to achieve the most effective carbon savings with the best financial payback.

Of course, lowering the impact of core business practice is fundamental to reducing our carbon emissions. What are the environmental practices of a company's suppliers? What investment decisions are being made? How efficient is the use of the raw materials employed?

But it isn't just about reducing carbon emissions, we must be prepared to adapt to the climate change that it is already too late to prevent. Workplaces will increasingly need to ensure there is sufficient shade outdoors, and blinds on windows to block the midday sun in summer. It might require more flexible working hours to get the best out of people on hot days, and it isn't just the heat – many of our buildings will be increasingly subjected to the risk of flash flooding, so will have to do their bit to reduce surface water run-off by having green roofs where appropriate, or even attenuating storm water on-site if possible.

'Going green' might be a buzzword, but there is no bigger challenge for this generation. If we're to be successful, it requires us all to take responsibility – individuals, businesses and government – and we can then pass on a planet of which we can be proud.

Members of the UK Green Building Council – consisting of businesses, small and large, from across the construction sector and related industries – are grappling with the challenge of climate change, and are committed to campaigning for a sustainable built environment and reducing their own impact. For more information go to www.ukgbc.org.

37 Energy performance certificates

From 2008, property owners must have an energy performance certificate for buildings over 540 sq ft, reports Charles Woollam at DTZ.

The European Commission wishes to reduce energy consumption in its member states through improving energy efficiency, partly as a means of reducing carbon emissions in accordance with the international Kyoto Treaty and partly in response to concerns over the long-term security of energy supplies.

It is hoped that, by labelling the energy efficiency of buildings, owners and occupiers will be able to reflect energy performance in pricing offers to buy and to lease commercial property.

The law

The Energy Performance of Buildings (Certificates and Inspections) (England & Wales) Regulations 2007 entered the statute books on 29 March 2007.

From 6 April 2008, property owners need to provide a copy of a valid Energy Performance Certificate for all new constructions and for existing buildings over 10,000 sq m (i.e. 107,080 sq ft) on any sale or leasing transaction. The later date of 1 July 2008 applies to buildings of over 2,500 sq m (27,000 sq ft) and, from 1 October 2008, the new regulations will apply to all buildings over 50 sq m (540 sq ft).

The certificate will record the energy performance of the building, benchmarked against similar buildings and will also include suggested improvements to energy efficiency. Assessed according to a prescribed method and presented in a standard format, each building will be given a rating from A (excellent) to G (very poor).

Certificates will last for a period of 10 years from issue, and it is worth noting that it is sufficient merely to provide a valid certificate on sales and lettings. There is currently no obligation to undertake any improvements, although this situation may clearly change over time.

Exemptions

Energy Performance Certificates will be required for most commercial buildings above 50 sq m (540 sq ft) other than those temporarily erected with an expected lifespan of less than two years and vacant buildings which are sold for demolition.

Some industrial buildings are also exempt but only where the air is neither heated nor cooled. Examples of qualifying industrial activities include hot processes, such as metal foundries, chemical processes, food and drinks packaging, and heavy engineering. The Regulations are slightly ambiguous but the exemption may not apply to warehouses, other than those used to store the output of heavy industrial processes.

Trigger date

New buildings require a certificate on physical completion of construction. Responsibility for providing the certificate lies with the constructor who must provide the certificate to the owner before Building Control will issue a final certificate of completion.

Existing buildings do not require a certificate until the time that they are first offered for sale or for rent, but free copies of certificates must be given to prospective buyers and tenants as soon as they first ask for information about the building or make a request to conduct a viewing. In practice, certificates will need to be in place before buildings are brought to market.

Whilst it is usually the responsibility of the seller or the landlord to provide the certificate, tenants should be aware that it is their responsibility to produce a certificate on assignment of a lease to a third party or on sub-letting. It is not necessary to provide a certificate on renewal of an existing lease.

Multi-let buildings

The Department for Communities and Local Government has issued a helpful Guide to Energy Performance Certificates, which sets out in some detail when one certificate is required for a whole building and when individual certificates are needed for each lettable part.

The basic rules are that residential units in a mixed use scheme will always require a separate certificate, prepared according to the standard methodology for domestic property and issued by an accredited domestic assessor. Where residential units are strictly ancillary to a prevailing commercial use and do not have separate access, the residential accommodation should be included in the commercial certificate.

For multi-let commercial property, owners and occupiers have a degree of choice; where buildings have shared services, it is possible to have a single certificate covering the entire property, which can be used on letting individual units or to have individual certificates covering each lettable part.

Where individual certificates are obtained, the certificate must include a proportion of any shared services or conditioned common areas, such as reception areas which must be assessed on a 'square metre basis' for the whole building.

Non-compliance

Responsibility for enforcing the Regulations has been given to Local Authority Trading Standards Officers who may request a copy of a valid certificate at any time within six months of it being required. Failure to provide a Trading Standards Officer with a valid certificate within seven days will attract a penalty of between £500 and £5,000, and is calculated with reference to the rateable value of the property.

Whilst the amount of the potential fine is relatively insignificant in comparison with the value of most transactions, the potential damage to corporate reputations from flouting laws designed to protect the environment is likely to act as a powerful incentive for responsible investors to comply.

Impact

Opinion is divided on whether the new Regulations will achieve their core objective of allowing potential occupiers and prospective purchasers of commercial property to price the relative energy efficiency of buildings into bids.

As a general rule, property values are influenced by a cornucopia of different factors. Now that energy efficiency is more easily identifiable, it is possible that inefficient buildings will come to trade at a discount, but the reality is that there is unlikely to be any great change in the market place.

In comparison with the key drivers of quality of location, quality of occupier and length of lease, energy efficiency will remain a minor issue. After all, more significant costs such as rates and service charges vary enormously between buildings but rarely have any impact on rental and capital value.

There are a number of practical difficulties. In a formal Impact Assessment prior to formalising the Regulations, for example, the UK Government significantly underestimated the number of Certificates required from 6 April 2008. Although transitional arrangements were hastily added in December 2007, progress in setting up the accreditation scheme for energy assessors has been painfully slow and accredited assessors are still in short supply.

To prevent any repetition of the botched introduction of Home Information Packs in the domestic sector, the Government has provided a 'get out of jail card' for owners and occupiers of commercial property. The DCLG Guide now effectively states that, provided an application is made at least 14 days prior to the required date and despite 'all reasonable efforts and enquiries' it has not been received, the applicant will be exempt from paying a fine for non-compliance.

Also, whilst landlords will have all the data required to enable the assessor to issue a Certificate, existing tenants of multi-let buildings, who will need a Certificate to offload surplus space, may have limited access to information about common areas and shared services, let alone floor areas needed to make an apportionment.

In the majority of cases, prudent landlords will elect to obtain copies of certificates covering the entire building, which tenants may then use, but this will not always be the case and there is an obvious mismatch on timing. Landlords will, after all, give priority to those buildings where they already have space to let and buildings ear-marked for sale. Tenants will soon become aggrieved in the event that unwanted accommodation cannot be brought to market through their landlord's delay.

Charles Woollam is a Chartered Surveyor and a Director of DTZ, one of the world's global real estate advisers. DTZ provides innovative real estate and business solutions worldwide. DTZ was one of the first property advisers to establish a dedicated Sustainability Team and has developed a range of services to help both owners and users of commercial property respond to various challenges of climate change. Charles Woollam 0207 408 1161 charles.woollam@dtz.com

Energy efficient windows...
They won't cost the earth

Did you know that 20% of all energy consumed in your home is lost through your windows.

Homes are responsible for 28% of all UK CO2 emissions; this is dramatic when compared to the 5.5% emitted by air travel.

Energy efficient windows help to contain and conserve heat within your home during the winter months and keep you cool in the summer.

New building regulations (2006) state that all new windows sold must conform to at least the lowest energy rating – 'E'.

To find out how energy efficient windows can help contact the British Fenestration Rating Council advice line today 020 7403 9200.

Registered through:
Glass and Glazing
Federation

British
Fenestration
Rating
Council

Glass and Glazing Federation

GGF
44-48 Borough High St | London | SE1 1XB
Tel | 0870 042 4255
Fax | 0870 042 4266
www.ggf.org.uk

38 Save money through better windows

Energy is disappearing fast out of the window, reports Liz Chapelhow of the Glass and Glazing Federation.

Are you maximising the energy savings you could make? You've fitted draught excluders, bought energy saving light bulbs, filled your cavity walls with insulation, turned down your central heating thermostat and insulated your loft.

But did you know that 20% of all energy consumed is lost through your windows?* That equates to 1.6 tonnes of carbon per year per home, which if you take the whole country means we are emitting as a nation 3.5 million tonnes of carbon in total and wasting £370 million.

Saving energy, saving money

If your property has single glazed windows – there is still a large number throughout the UK – then there are significant savings you could make by installing what are known as Energy Efficient Windows. Even if you have double glazed windows they may not be as energy efficient as they could be, especially if they were installed prior to April 2002. All of this means we are not being as energy efficient as we could be in our homes and they are emitting unnecessary amounts of carbon or CO_2 and its costing us more in our energy bills.

As we all know, the emission of CO_2 into the atmosphere is creating global warming. In the UK our use of energy in homes and offices is becoming more critical and attention is being focused on how energy efficient our buildings really are. Research shows that 23% of lost energy from buildings is through windows and doors.

If your windows are inefficient you will inevitably have high energy bills and will be paying to heat the planet, rather than your property.

Some killer facts

1. Average yearly energy bill savings made from installing Energy Efficient Windows in a typical UK House:

    *   A single glazed house – £150.49*
    *   A double glazed house – £44.88

    Up to £461 saved in an electrically-heated house.

2. Current annual CO_2 emissions from an average dwelling are 1.6 tonnes.

    *   Energy Efficient Windows would reduce the carbon footprint of a typical single-glazed dwelling by 0.30 tonnes, ie 19%.
    *   Energy Efficient Windows would reduce the carbon footprint of a typical double-glazed dwelling by 0.09 tonnes, ie 6%.

    2,516,986 tonnes of carbon.

    9,228,950 tonnes of CO_2.

3. Converting ALL existing windows to Energy Efficient Windows would save the UK each year:

    *   £2,363 million
    *   3,970,663 tonnes of carbon
    *   14,559,098 tonnes of CO_2.

4. UK expenditure on household fuel and power in 2006 was £22,726 million; therefore Energy Efficient Windows would reduce national domestic energy expenditure by 10%.

5. Installing solar control glass in all new and existing air-conditioned buildings would save the UK:

    *   1,097,000 tonnes of CO_2.

6. However, if the use of air-conditioning grows to the same level of penetration in 2020 as currently exists in the USA, putting solar control glass in all new and existing air-conditioned buildings would save the UK:

    *   6,882,000 tonnes of CO_2.

    (Correct at time of going to press.)

With such astonishing figures in mind it should now be clear as to the potential contribution the glass and glazing industry can make to a 'greener' environment.

What Are Energy Efficient Windows?

They are windows that will help to contain and conserve heat within your property during the winter, cool it in the summer, keep out wind and resist condensation. They will save you money on your energy bills and reduce your carbon footprint – something we are all being asked to do.

From 2006 new Building Regulations have meant that all windows sold must conform to at least the lowest energy efficiency rating – 'E". In the UK windows are rated according to a colour bar chart system similar to the ones seen on household goods (washing machines, tumble dryers etc) in shops throughout the country.

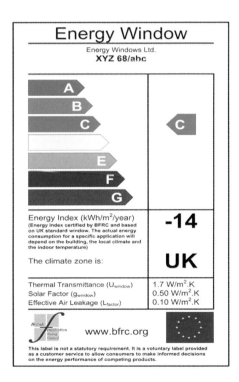

Energy saving ratings

These energy ratings are controlled and awarded by the British Fenestration Rating Council (BFRC) which is owned by the fenestration and glazing industries trade association – the Glass and Glazing Federation (GGF). All window manufacturers can apply to BFRC to get their windows tested for ratings A-G, with 'A' being the most energy efficient and 'E' the least – for more information on the BFRC and its energy ratings system visit the website, www.bfrc.org or telephone their advice line, 020 7403 9200.

Carbon calculator

Your local GGF member window installer is about to make decision making a whole lot easier when choosing Energy Efficient Windows.

The GGF has developed a 'carbon calculator' that will be used by its Members from January 2008 onwards. It will allow your window installer to input details about your property and its existing windows – plus house, bungalow or flat 'type', what fuel you use and its unit cost and lastly the Energy Efficient Windows you are thinking about having fitted. It will then calculate how much energy and money you will save for each grade of replacement window.

But its only GGF member companies that will have this 'carbon calculator'. To make sure your window fitter is a GGF member look in your local phone book (most members advertise their membership by using the GGF logo in their ads). Alternatively you can go to the GGF website – www.ggf.co.uk – where you can get a full list of member companies in your area.

The Glass and Glazing Federation (GGF) is the recognised leading authority and voice for employers and companies within the flat glass, glazing, window, home improvement, plastics and applied window film industries in the UK. With members in over 1,000 business locations – there is a GGF member in almost every UK town.

Our members work across the industry from emergency glazing, applied film, conservatories, windows, doors, fire resistant glazing, glazing components, flat glass, curtain walling, mirrors, toughened glass, curved glass, extrusions, hardware, glass merchanting, insulated glass and laminated glass

The Federation provides a technical consultancy service. For further information and details of costs contact the Glass and Glazing Federation.

For further information on Energy Efficient Windows see the British Fenestration Rating Council website www.bfrc.org.uk or ring the advice line on 020 7403 9200.

TrustMark is an initiative between Government, consumer groups and industry designed to help people find reputable firms to do repair, maintenance and improvement work in the home www.trustmark.org.uk

Further details: Glass and Glazing Federation, 44-48 Borough High Street, London SE1 1XB
Tel: 0870 042 4255
Fax: 0870 042 4266
e-mail info@ggf.org.uk www.ggf.org.uk

LED Lighting Specialist

Long Life Reliability
does not cost the earth

LED Product Range

NEW LED MR16
Halogen lamp replacement

- Reduce electricity consumption by up to 80%

- Reduce Air Conditioning requirement thanks to low temperature light beam

- Reduce maintenance costs with lamp life in excess of 50,000 hours

- Improve reliability

- Improve staff and customer environment

- Choice of light output colours

- Standard or bespoke solutions

- A truly GREEN solution to your lighting requirements

Decorative Lighting

Handrail Lighting

For a solution to your special requirements please contact:

**LPA Excil Electronics Ripley Drive
Normanton West Yorkshire WF6 1QT
Tel: +44 (0)1924 224100 Fax: 01924 224111
e-mail: enquiries@lpa-excil.com**

www.lpa-group.com

39 LED lighting technology

Long lasting and cheap to run. John Hesketh at LPA-Excil
Electronics reviews a breakthrough in lighting.

The light emitting diode (LED) is currently revolutionising the lighting
industry. From a lighting perspective, it is the first major step forward in
illumination technology since the fluorescent lamp became commercially
available in the 1950's.

Historically, LEDs have been associated only with indication applications,
but rapid and recent advances in the technology have transformed the device
from these historical applications to a viable source of general illumination.

Without dispute, the main technological advance has been in the area of
significantly improved luminous efficacy measured in lumens per watt
(lm/w). It has been this improvement that has resulted in today's high output
power LEDs which have permitted the requirements of the illumination
market to be addressed.

Development is ongoing with improvements by the major LED manufacturers published virtually monthly. Interest from the lighting market is
escalating as the huge potential benefits such as ultra long service life and
low energy consumption among many other advantages are realised.

The technology

Unlike any other conventional light source, the LED is a fully solid state
device. This means that light is produced by a semiconductor junction rather
than relying on filaments or gas discharge processes. This makes the device
extremely robust and ideally suited for high reliability markets.

The first LED was created in the early 1920's although the development
work at this time was not officially reported. It was not until the mid 1950's
that official scientific reports began to emerge. In 1962, the first practical

visible light spectrum LED was perfected with red emission colour and subsequently, yellow and green spectral colours followed.

The development of the first blue LED resulted in a quick progression to the first white light LED when it was discovered that adding a yellow phosphor coating over the blue light resulted in white light.

Historically, LEDs have been associated only with indication applications, but rapid and recent advances in the technology have transformed the device from these historical applications to a viable source of general illumination.

Around 1999, power LEDs were introduced to the market place capable of continuous operation of up to 1 watt. Such devices operate at very high luminous efficacy and are serious contenders for illumination applications. Soon after initial introduction of the power LED, devices were introduced with even higher continuous power ratings and 3 and 5 watt devices became commonplace.

The major LED manufacturers are now placing emphasis on improvement of luminous efficacy rather than on producing higher power devices. Power LED efficacy levels have improved from initial values of 18 lm/w to well in excess of 100 lm/w. Rather than having several different devices capable of 1, 3 and 5 watt operation, manufacturers have tended to standardise on a common device which can be driven as required up to a maximum power of around 4 watts.

Life expectancy and disposal

Life expectancy of an LED system is critically dependent upon correct thermal design. Assuming this is optimal, typical life expectancies range between 30,000 and 100,000 hours. In comparison, this compares to 1,000 to 3,000 hours for halogen lamps and 10,000 to 20,000 hours for standard fluorescent lamps.

When discussing the life expectancy of LEDs, it is important to understand that figures quoted generally relate to lumen maintenance or put simply, the time to which the lumen output is expected to be 70% of the initial value, such a decrease in light output is not generally discernable to the naked eye. The most common way for an LED to fail is by gradual reduction in lumen output due to loss of luminous efficacy. Sudden loss of light output due to short or open circuit failure can occur but is very rare. It should also be noted that LED life is unaffected by frequent on-off cycling, unlike fluorescent and halogen lamps where this has a negative effect on lamp life.

These outstanding life expectancy figures enable the implementation of low life cycle cost lighting installations. Maintenance costs are virtually eradicated as is the requirement for stock-holding of lamp spares. Often a true 'fit and forget' solution is realised for typically 12 years.

The long life properties result in a secondary benefit which is elimination of lamp disposals and associated costs, with the obvious benefits to the environment. When the LED system does eventually fail and disposal is imminent, the environmental impact is minimised as LEDs are RoHS compliant and contain no chlorofluorocarbons (CFCs), persistent organic pollutants (POPs), volatile organic compounds (VOCs), halogen, mercury or harmful chemicals.

Reduced energy consumption

The first power LED introduced to the market place offered a luminous efficacy of around 18 lumens/watt (lm/w). Around 2006 this improved to 50 to 60 lm/w and by 2007, the 100 lm/w target figure had been reached. The 100 lm/w figure had always been regarded as the target, as this is the luminous efficacy level typically attained by a high quality triphosphor fluorescent lamp.

To put the LED efficacy levels in perspective, it is worth noting that a conventional incandescent lamp as typically used within the home operates at just 10 lm/w. Halogen lamps offer better luminous efficacy at around 15 to 20 lm/w but this is still significantly below the values attainable from current technology LEDs.

As a practical example, LPA-Excil Electronics has developed an LED version of the popular MR16 halogen lamp. This unit contains three LEDs each driven at 1 watt, all necessary optics and associated drive electronics for compatibility with the usual 12V AC or DC nominal low voltage distribution system. The arrangement produces equivalent light output to that of a 20W halogen type but consumes just 4.5 watts. This represents a 77% energy saving.

The low energy consumption benefit has huge implications for battery maintained emergency lighting systems where illumination periods can be significantly extended or battery ratings can be down-sized resulting in more compact luminaire designs.

Cool beam temperature

Unlike incandescent or halogen lamps, LEDs do not emit infra red or ultraviolet radiation. This results in cool beam temperature. It is not uncommon for the front glass temperature of a halogen MR16 to reach in excess of 90 degrees C, in comparison an LED equivalent would typically be less than a third of this.

This has obvious human factor implications, for example retail display or reading light applications where the sheer beam heat resulting from a conventional halogen solution can be very uncomfortable.

There is also a secondary effect and that is the potential savings on air conditioning operating costs. Because the beam temperature is much reduced, the heating effect of the surrounding ambient is significantly reduced; this in turn results in less required effort from the air conditioning systems with inherent energy savings.

Robust solution

Because the device utilises semiconductor technology, there are no fragile filaments or gas discharge process to fail, this makes the device immune from the effects of shock and vibration. The device is therefore ideally suited to transport, and other high reliability markets where traditional halogen solutions have proved problematic. Other examples include hazardous areas and applications where access is difficult or limited.

A property of power LED technology is that light output is inversely proportional to temperature, i.e. light output increases as temperature falls. This characteristic makes LEDs ideally suited to low temperature environments such as cold rooms and refrigeration applications. This is just the opposite of fluorescent technology where light output falls off rapidly below around 10 degrees C.

Electrical and thermal considerations

The LED is a more complicated device to drive electrically than a conventional incandescent or halogen lamp as it requires a current regulated power supply. With a conventional lamp, a voltage is applied to the filament and the lamp draws a current dependent upon the filament resistance.

An LED requires drive with a regulated current. When this current passes through the device, a voltage is developed which dependent upon the LED type is usually between 1.2 and 4.5V. Because the LEDs are current fed, the usual method of feeding several devices from a common current regulated power supply is by connecting in series. This differs to conventional lamps which would be connected in parallel.

This gives rise to the requirement for specialist LED power supply units or 'control gear'. These power supplies must accept at their input the required system operating voltage including tolerance variation ranges and produce, at their output, the necessary regulated current. For power LEDs, a typical current would be around 350mA.

There are two approaches to the power supply requirement, the first is to integrate this into the luminaire or light fitting and the second is to have a remotely located power supply unit capable of driving a number of light heads. The latter solution is more cost effective where large numbers of light heads are required.

For drop-in LED replacements for halogen lamps such as MR16, it is more convenient to integrate the power supply within the lamp such that it forms a true 'drop-in' replacement. The LED solution can then be driven at, for example, 12V even though the LEDs themselves are operating at a constant current.

One point to note is that the series connection can result in loss of a number of light heads in the event of open circuit failure, so it is prudent to include some form of trip circuit which activates and maintains the circuit in the event of device open circuit.

From a thermal perspective, the LED semiconductor junction dissipates power. This is more of an issue with today's power LEDs than in older gallium arsenide indicator types. The heat must be effectively routed away from the semiconductor junction as LED life expectancy is inversely related to temperature.

In order to reduce junction temperature, good thermal design or 'heat sinking' is required. High power LEDs are mounted to thermally optimised printed circuit boards which have an aluminium substrate, these are then in turn mounted to heat sinks. The heat sinking can be attained in a number of ways, one of which is to utilise the fitting metal work but more conventional heat sinks such as those commonly found in electronic equipment are often used. For multi LED arrays, significant heat sinking is required.

A point of note which stresses the importance of thermal design is that a rise in junction temperature from 60 to 80 degrees C would typically halve LED life from 100,000 to 50,000 hours.

Optical considerations

The LED is a small area light source. High power LEDs generally have a large light emission angle, typically 110 degrees. In order to produce a usable light beam, carefully designed secondary optics are required to collect, focus and collimate the light output from the LED.

In practical terms, the secondary optic generally sits over the LED and locates onto the thermal printed circuit board to which the LED itself is mounted.

Secondary optics are available with differing beam angles and beam shapes. The most common types offer round beams but elliptical and strip are available. For circular beams, there is a choice of differing beam angles, typically 12, 30 and 45 degrees equating to traditional spot, medium and flood definitions.

Lenses vary considerably in efficiency, a great deal of available luminous flux can be lost during the focussing process if the design is not optimum. Generally, simple lenses are very poor in efficiency returning figures of only 50%, but more involved total internal reflection designs can offer efficiency levels as high as 90%. High lens efficiency levels are important in order to fully realise the true potential of LEDs.

Generally lenses have specified lens factors which are given in units of candelas per lumen (cd/lm). This enables luminous intensity to be calculated, which in turn permits an illumination level in lux to be calculated by dividing the luminous intensity by the square of the distance from source. Generally speaking, illumination calculations for LED systems are reasonably accurate.

Colour availability and colour temperature

LEDs are available in a wide variety of spectral output colours; red, yellow, green, blue and white are readily available. LEDs are even available with red, green and blue devices in a single package permitting colour mixing.

A common complaint of LEDs historically has been emphasised blue content of white light LEDs. The industry now has this under control with a system known as colour binning, which permits a given colour temperature to be specified.

White LEDs are typically available in three distinct colour bands these being warm white (2650 to 3500K), natural white (3500 to 4500K) and cool white (4500 to 6500K). Additionally it is possible to narrow down within a range as each category in sub-divided into colour bins. It is, therefore, possible to implement a very consistent lighting system with colour temperature matching that of incandescent and fluorescent systems where necessary.

Conclusions

With luminous efficacy figures in excess of 100 lm/w, LEDs are now serious contenders for general illumination and utility lighting schemes.

It is clear that LEDs have great potential to realise significantly reduced life cycle cost illumination systems due to their inherent high reliability characteristics. Case studies for railway rolling stock applications have demonstrated pay back periods as short as two years, and fit and forget installations for typically 12 to 13 years.

The huge potential savings in energy consumption, coupled with radical reductions in lamp disposals offer huge environmental benefits. When disposal is eventually required, the LED material content ensures minimal environmental impact.

The cool beam temperature contributes considerably to a more comfortable illuminated environment with a further secondary energy saving associated with reduced air conditioning requirements.

John Hesketh is technical director at LPA-Excil Electronics. His area of speciality is analogue and power electronics design and rail vehicle interior lighting systems. The majority of the electronics design work has been high reliability rolling stock focussed, including products such as high frequency inverters, switched mode power supplies and various control and monitoring applications. Now in charge of engineering design and development activities at LPA-Excil Electronics, John runs a department specialising in rolling stock electronics and innovative interior lighting system design with emphasis on LED technology. He graduated in Electrical and Electronic Engineering from Leeds Metropolitan University in 1983. Further details from:

John Hesketh, Technical Director, LPA-Excil Electronics, Ripley Drive, Normanton WF6 1QT

E-mail: j.hesketh@lpa-excil.com

Tel: 01924 224100